HOW TO FREE YOUR MIND
Tara the Liberator

How to Free Your Mind

Tara the Liberator

Bhikshuni Thubten Chodron

SNOW LION PUBLICATIONS

ITHACA, NEW YORK • BOULDER, COLORADO

Snow Lion Publications
P.O. Box 6483
Ithaca, NY 14851 USA
(607) 273-8519
www.snowlionpub.com

Text designed and typeset by Gopa & Ted2, Inc.
Illustrations by Peter Green
Printed in Canada on acid-free recycled paper.

ISBN 1-55939-226-6

Library of Congress Cataloging-in-Publication Data

Thubten Chodron, 1950–
   How to free your mind : Tara the liberator /
Bhikshuni Thubten Chodron.
      p. cm.
   Includes bibliographical references.
   ISBN 1-55939-226-6 (alk. paper)
   1. Tārā (Goddess) I. Title
BQ4710.T3T49 2005
294.3'42114 — dc22
                              2004025255

Contents

ALSO BY THUBTEN CHODRON

Buddhism for Beginners (Snow Lion Publications)

Glimpse of Reality (with Dr. Alexander Berzin)

Guided Meditations on the Lamrim, the Gradual Path to Enlightenment (set of 14 CDs) (Dharma Friendship Foundation)

Open Heart, Clear Mind (Snow Lion Publications)

Taming the Mind (Snow Lion Publications)

The Path to Happiness (Texas Buddhist Association)

Working with Anger (Snow Lion Publications)

The Yoga Method of Chenresig (FPMT Education Dept.)

BOOKS EDITED BY THUBTEN CHODRON

A Chat about Heruka, by Lama Zopa Rinpoche (Lama Yeshe Wisdom Archives)

A Chat about Yamantaka, by Lama Zopa Rinpoche (Lama Yeshe Wisdom Archives)

Blossoms of the Dharma: Living as a Buddhist Nun (North Atlantic Books, Berkeley CA)

Choosing Simplicity: A Commentary on the Bhikshuni Pratimoksha, by Ven. Bhikshuni Master Wu Yin (Snow Lion Publications)

Heruka Body Mandala: Sadhana and Commentary, by Ven. Lati Rinpoche

Interfaith Insights (Timeless Books, New Delhi)

Pearl of Wisdom, Book I and II: Buddhist Prayers and Practices (Sravasti Abbey)

Transforming the Heart: The Buddhist Way to Joy and Courage, by Geshe Jampa Tegchok (Snow Lion Publications)

Preface

My guru Serkong Tsenshab Rinpoche, who was also a guru of His Holiness the Dalai Lama, said that praying to Tara makes it is easy to be reborn in the pure land of Avalokiteshvara, the Buddha of Compassion, and receive guidance from him. This is because Tara is close to sentient beings in the way that a mother is close to her children.

If you put your full trust in Tara, you will receive the guidance you need and all your problems will be solved, especially those that relate to each of the Twenty-one Taras, each of whom manifested to alleviate specific problems. Therefore, each of these Taras exists for you.

Even I have experience of this. I once gave the practice of the Twenty-one Taras to a student who had terminal cancer, and with the help of Tara he recovered completely and became a well-known healer.

However, it is your practice of the good heart—cherishing and serving others—that really brings Tara close to you. This is what pleases her most and allows her always to guide you.

Still, the Twenty-one Taras do not exist mainly for temporal success and healing but for the ultimate purpose of freeing you from all sufferings—such as the cycle of aging, sickness, death and rebirth, dissatisfaction, relationship problems and so forth—and their cause: delusion and karma and the negative imprints they leave on your mental continuum, and bringing you to the ever-lasting happiness of liberation and full enlightenment.

Practicing the teachings contained in this book with the intention of reaching liberation and enlightenment will definitely lead you there.

Lama Zopa Rinpoche

Introduction

EVER SINCE Lama Thubten Yeshe first introduced me to the meditation practice of Green Tara in 1975, I was attracted to this Buddha. Although all Buddhas have the same realizations, Tara's appearance was very friendly and welcoming. While my mind would sometimes project its self-created authority issues on other Buddhas, admitting my imperfections to Tara didn't bother me. Fortunately, I gradually came to feel this way about other enlightened ones, too. Lama Yeshe later explained that most Tibetan Buddhists feel close to Tara; in fact, to indicate his own affection, he called her "Mummy Tara."

This book is written with that affection. Tara's meditation practice has helped me through many ups and downs in my life and in my Dharma practice. My wish is to share my understanding of Tara with you in the hopes that it will help you to understand more clearly your own mind and its potential. Tara is a manifestation of what each of us can become, and as such, she shows us good qualities to cultivate on the path to enlightenment as well as obstacles to abandon.

How to Free Your Mind: Tara the Liberator is directed toward a general audience. One need not be a Buddhist to read it or gain something from it. If you are curious about Buddhist deities, if you want to learn how to free your mind from disturbing emotions such as clinging attachment and anger, if you wonder what the nature of reality is, if you are interested in female Buddhas, you will find something of interest in these pages.

Chapter 1 introduces Tara and discusses her symbolism and the various ways in which we can view her. Chapter 2 describes the purpose of meditating on Tara and the important elements of a *sadhana*—or guided meditation—on Tara. Here we learn about refuge in the Three Jewels, the loving and compassionate motivation of *bodhichitta*, and how to visualize Green Tara and recite her mantra. Tara's name means "liberator," and she is said to liberate us from eight internal and eight external dangers. She does this by teaching us the ways to tame our mind so that we are not constantly befuddled by pride, ignorance, anger, jealousy, distorted views, miserliness, attachment, and doubt. Chapter 3 explains this. Chapter 4 is the "Homage to the Twenty-one Taras," praises to Tara that are frequently chanted in Tibetan monasteries and homes, and chapter 5 contains the explanation of the "Homage" and the twenty-one manifestations of Tara. After reciting the "Homage," people often chant some verses describing the benefits of reciting it. These verses and their explanation are found in chapter 6.

Chapter 7 contains one of my favorite poems, "A Song of Longing for Tara, the Infallible," written by Lama Lobsang Tenpey Gyaltsen when he was only eighteen or nineteen years old. My reflections on this moving poem are found in chapter 8. The song gives us wise advice for Dharma practice, and following it brings us closer to Tara. Chapters 9 and 10 discuss Tara's ultimate nature, her emptiness of inherent existence. Her ultimate nature and ours are the same, and to the extent that we realize emptiness, the afflictions obscuring our mind evaporate and we approach Tara's enlightened state.

A glossary of important terms and a list of additional reading are resources for you to explore.

This book is written in a conversational style. Most of the chapters began as talks that I gave to people from Dharma Friendship Foundation, a Buddhist center in Seattle. Most were transcribed and lightly edited by Ven. Tenzin Tsepal; others were done by Jesse Fenton and Toby Steers. I then worked on them again, before Ven. Tsepal proofread the final manuscript. Dechen Rochard checked chapters 9 and 10. I appreciate their help very much.

My gratitude to all my teachers who taught me not only the meditation practice of Tara, but also the gradual path to enlightenment. Among these are His Holiness the Dalai Lama, Tsenzhap Serkong Rinpoche, Lama Zopa

Rinpoche, Lama Thubten Yeshe, Geshe Jampa Tegchok, and others. Whatever benefit comes from this book is due to their kindness and to the kindness of all those who supported me while I worked on the manuscript. All mistakes are my own.

Bhikshuni Thubten Chodron

Sravasti Abbey

June 3, 2004

Who is Tara?

B EFORE YOU, sitting on a lotus, is a beautiful young woman with a body of green radiating light. Who is she? What is Tara? Why do practitioners of Tibetan Buddhism meditate upon such a being? How can a spiritual relationship with her enrich our lives?

WHAT IS A BUDDHA?

Tara is a Buddha. Anybody who has become a Buddha—and there are many Buddhas—has an omniscient mind. The qualities of all these enlightened ones are the same. Buddhas have eliminated all defilements, both afflictive obscurations that keep us locked in cyclic existence—ignorance, anger, attachment, and the karma that causes cyclic existence—and cognitive obscurations—the subtle stains or predispositions of afflictions on the mind and the appearance of inherent existence that they cause. Any Buddha has totally abandoned everything to be abandoned and completely developed all good qualities, such as equanimity, love, compassion, joy, and the six far-reaching attitudes—generosity, ethical discipline, patience, joyous effort, concentration, and wisdom.

Tara, like Manjushri, Avalokiteshvara, Vajrapani, and others, is a Buddha. A Buddha is not a creator God. A Buddha does not manage the universe, controlling sentient beings' destiny, rewarding some and punishing others. Those of us who were not raised Buddhist can easily bring our previous religious conditioning into Buddhist practice and substitute Buddha for God. Since this would create many difficulties in our spiritual practice, let's be careful to avoid it.

For example, one part of us may hold a child-like Sunday school conception of God as an old man in the sky, who sometimes is benevolent and at other times jealous and wrathful. We must be careful not to impute those qualities onto a Buddha. Tara is not a concrete, self-existent person with a personality, and for this reason, we train our minds to see her as an emanation of all the good qualities that we admire and want to cultivate. This gives us a different feeling.

A Buddha has two main bodies: a *dharmakaya* or truth body, and a *rupakaya* or form body. Here, "body" doesn't mean physical body but a collection of qualities. The omniscient mind—the fully enlightened mind that has eliminated all defilements and realized all good qualities—is the dharmakaya. The rupakaya or form body allows a Buddha to communicate with beings who are not yet Buddhas. Because our minds are obscured, we cannot directly know the Buddha's omniscient mind, and so the Buddhas appear in various forms out of compassion in order to benefit us. All of the different forms in which a Buddha appears are called form bodies.

Form bodies are further divided into two types. The *sambhogakaya*, or enjoyment body, is a body made of light that is found in the pure lands. The enjoyment body is the form that a Buddha takes to teach high-level bodhisattvas. The *nirmanakaya*, or emanation body, is the form that a Buddha takes when he appears in our impure world. For example, Shakyamuni Buddha appeared as a historical person nearly 2,600 years ago. He was a nirmanakaya Buddha, an emanation body manifesting as a monk giving teachings in ancient India. A modern-day example of an emanation body is His Holiness the Dalai Lama. Many people believe that the Dalai Lama is a fully enlightened being, even though it's impossible for us to prove this at our limited stage of spiritual development. Out of compassion, in order to benefit us, Buddhas manifest in our world and appear to us as ordinary beings in forms that resemble ours. They may seem to have ups and downs in life just as we do, but internally they do not experience confusion and turmoil because they have eliminated all causes of suffering.

A bodhisattva is someone training to become a Buddha. This person is fired by bodhichitta, the aspiration to become fully enlightened in order to benefit all beings most effectively. The primary reason a bodhisattva works so hard to purify and cultivate her mind is to benefit all beings. After becoming enlightened, bodhisattvas manifest in different forms in order to communicate with us. If they didn't, they wouldn't be able to fulfill their purpose. Someone doesn't work for three countless great eons to become enlightened and then just relax and go to sleep! Instead, enlightened activities spontaneously and effortlessly flow from that pure state. These activities will naturally be beneficial, because they stem from an altruistic motivation coupled with deep wisdom.

Tara can be understood on many different levels. First, she is a historical figure, a person who generated bodhichitta—the altruistic intention to attain full enlightenment in order to benefit all living beings most effectively—and then actualized that intention by becoming a Buddha. Second, she is a manifestation of awakened qualities; and third, she is our Buddha-potential in its future fully purified and evolved form. We may alternate between these understandings, using them as needed to cultivate our good qualities.

TARA AS A PERSON

Many eons ago in a different universe lived a princess named Yeshe Dawa. Based on her own investigation and experience, she had great confidence in the Three Jewels the Buddha, Dharma, and Sangha. She understood the unsatisfactory nature of cyclic existence and thus determined to be free from all sufferings. Thinking that all living beings were like her in wanting happiness and not wanting suffering, Princess Yeshe Dawa developed genuine, impartial love and compassion for each and every living being. She was not enchanted by the luxuries of palace life; instead, she vowed to show the way to liberation to millions of beings each day before eating breakfast, to millions more before eating lunch, and to even more before going to sleep at night. Because of this, she was called Arya Tara (Tib: *Pagma Drolma*), meaning the "noble liberator." *Arya* indicates that she has directly realized the nature of reality and *Tara* shows her liberating activity. When the religious authorities of that place suggested that she pray to be reborn as a man in future lives, Tara refused, pointing out that many Buddhas had already manifested in male bodies. She vowed to attain full enlightenment in a woman's body and continuously to return in female form in order to benefit others.

Whether we're men or women, this historical Tara is a role model for us. Just like us, she was once an ordinary being with problems, stress, and disturbing emotions. But by training her mind in the Buddha's teachings, she attained full enlightenment. Likewise, if we practice the Dharma with joyful effort, we too can attain her state. Smiling at us, Tara says, "If I can do it, so can you!" thus encouraging us along the path.

In another legend, Tara is said to have been born from Avalokiteshvara's tear. As a bodhisattva, Avalokiteshvara (Tib: *Chenresig*; Chin: *Kuan Yin*) worked diligently to free all beings from the hell realms. Having done this, he rested a while; but when he awoke, he found the hells completely repopulated with sentient beings born there by the power of their harmful actions. For a moment he despaired and began to weep with sorrow for the plight of these ignorant beings. From one of his tears, Tara emerged and encouraged him on the bodhisattva path, saying, "Do not despair. I will help you to liberate all beings."

In this story, we again see Tara as a person, one with a miraculous birth. This legend can inspire us not to lose faith in the arduous process of benefiting beings. Such patience and perseverance are necessary for as we know, ignorant beings such as we are at present often do the opposite of what brings happiness and peace. Tara's optimism gives us strength in difficult situations through showing us that suffering can be overcome.

TARA AS A MANIFESTATION OF ENLIGHTENED QUALITIES

A second way to understand Tara is as a manifestation or embodiment of enlightened qualities. Anyone who has attained Buddhahood can appear in the form of any of the deities. There isn't just one Green Tara, or Thousand-Armed Avalokiteshvara, or one Manjushri, or one Vajrapani. These are simply appearances, emanations.

A Buddha's mind is beyond our present limited perceptual or conceptual abilities. All enlightened beings practiced for eons to purify their minds and enhance their capabilities in order to benefit us. But they need a way to communicate with us to lead us on the path out of suffering to full enlightenment. Since we are embodied beings who relate to color, shape, and other objects of the senses, the compassionate Buddhas appear in various forms in order to communicate with us. Tara, like other meditation deities, is one of those forms.

Each deity is a manifestation of the same enlightened qualities—love, compassion, joy, equanimity, generosity, ethical discipline, patience, enthusiasm, concentration, wisdom, and so forth—although each manifestation may emphasize a particular quality. For example, Tara symbolizes enlightened activity, while Avalokiteshvara embodies compassion. Among the diverse forms of Tara, Green Tara, who will be described below, eliminates obstacles and brings success. White Tara counteracts illness and bestows long life. Each of the 21 Taras and 108 Taras has her own specialty, symbolized by her color, implements, and physical posture.

Tara is an emanation of bliss and emptiness. Within the sphere of emptiness—the absence of inherent existence—blissful wisdom realizing emptiness appears in the form of Tara. By appearing in this physical form of Tara, the wisdom of bliss and emptiness of all Buddhas inspires us to cultivate constructive attitudes and actions. By understanding the symbolic meaning of Tara's physical characteristics, we gain confidence in and are moved to follow the path she teaches, generating her qualities within ourselves.

If we think about the qualities of a Buddha, how would those qualities look if they appeared in color, shape, and form? Even though all Buddhas have the same internal traits and qualities, they appear in different manifestations to emphasize certain characteristics. For example, an artist or a musician has an internal feeling or meaning he wants to express. In order to communicate it, he draws a picture with color and shape or creates a symphony with sound to express what's going on inside. In a similar way, Buddhas express their realizations in different external forms.

When we look at Tara, what kind of feeling does Tara give us? Think of Tara and think of George W. Bush. Do you get a different feeling when you think about each of them? Visualizing George Bush gives us a certain kind of energy. Visualizing Tara generates a very different kind of energy in us.

Her female form draws us into spiritual life. My teacher, Lama Thubten Yeshe, who practiced Tara meditation daily, often referred to her as "Mummy Tara." Just as most of us worldly beings feel affinity for our mothers and rely on their constant, compassionate help, we are naturally attracted to Tara's female appearance. We can relax in her presence and look at ourselves honestly, knowing that Tara will not judge, reject, or abandon us due to our shortcomings. Like a mother, she sees her child's potential—in this case, our spiritual potential or Buddha-nature—and wants to nurture it. We feel that we can easily entrust ourselves to the path she teaches. In this way her female form functions to increase our confidence in the Three Jewels and to feel supported in our practice.

Her female form represents wisdom, the essential element needed to remove the ignorance that misconstrues reality and is the root of all our suffering. Women tend to have quick, intuitive, and comprehensive understanding. Tara represents this quality and consequently can help us to develop such wisdom. Thus she is called "the mother of all the Buddhas," for the wisdom realizing reality that she embodies gives birth to full enlightenment, the state of freedom from self-grasping ignorance and its attendant, self-centeredness.

Green Tara's color symbolizes activity and success. Although she possesses the same qualities as other manifestations of the omniscient ones, she specifically embodies the enlightening influence by which the Buddhas act to benefit and guide us. In addition, she represents the purified aspect of the element of air, which activates growth in the world. Just as the air element generates the growth of green plants, which consequently brings the uplifted spirit of springtime after the dreariness of winter, Tara's enlightening influence makes our good qualities bloom and leads us to the freshness of liberation after the oppression of cyclic existence.

Lush green plants that grow easily are a farmer's delight. Similarly, her green color represents success—in worldly affairs as well as in spiritual development—giving us a sense of delight, hope, and optimism. Aspirations made in the presence of Green Tara may easily grow into results, and requests made to her may be quickly actualized. One reason for this is that by visualizing and praying to Tara, we are energized to create causes for happiness and to eliminate interferences in our Dharma practice.

Tara's body is made of light. Transparent, it appears and yet is intangible, like a rainbow, mirage, or illusion. In this way, her body represents the compatibility of the two truths: conventional and ultimate. On the conventional level, Tara appears and exists. Yet when we search for her ultimate mode of existence, we cannot find anything that exists inherently, independent from causes and conditions, parts, and terms and concepts. Tara conventionally appears, like an illusion, but ultimately cannot be found and is empty of an inherent essence.

Tara's body language expresses her inner realizations and outer activities. She doesn't sit with her head down or with her arms crossed in front of her chest as we do when we are closed or moody. Rather, her "dancing posture" is relaxed, open, and friendly. Her outstretched right foot indicates her readiness to step into the realms of suffering, confused beings in order to help us. Due to her altruistic intention, Tara can appear in these realms without being adversely affected by the environment. She doesn't shy away from suffering but faces it fearlessly and compassionately, thereby counteracting it. Her left leg is tucked in, demonstrating that she has full control over her subtle inner energies. No matter whether others praise or blame her, harm or help her, her energy does not become unbalanced and she does not lose her equanimity.

Tara's right hand in the gesture of granting sublime realizations shows that by following the path we can attain these realizations ourselves. This gesture is also called the gesture of generosity, symbolizing her willingness to give material possessions, love, protection, and the Dharma to all beings according to their needs and their dispositions. Her left hand is in the gesture of the Three Jewels, with the thumb and ring finger touching and the other three fingers stretched upward. These three fingers represent the Three Jewels. They indicate that by entrusting ourselves to these three objects of refuge and practicing their teachings, we can actualize the unity of compassionate bliss and wisdom, which is symbolized by the joining of her ring finger and thumb.

Tara's right hand and foot are both extended outward, emphasizing her compassionate activity—the method aspect of the path to enlightenment. Her left hand and foot, which are closer to her, indicate her imperturbable inner peace, gained through practicing the wisdom aspect of the path.

In each hand, Tara holds the stems of *utpala*, or blue lotus, flowers. On her left side, one utpala is a bud, one is blossoming, and one is fully open. The bud represents the Buddhas of the future, the fully opened lotus symbolizes the Buddhas of the past, and the blossoming lotus is the Buddhas of the present.

On Tara's crown is Amitabha Buddha, peaceful and smiling. As Tara's spiritual mentor, he represents the importance of having a fully qualified, wise, and compassionate guide on the path. By keeping her mentor on her crown, Tara is ever mindful of the teachings she has received from him. This reminds us to do the same.

While we ordinary beings decorate ourselves with external ornaments to look beautiful, Tara's inner beauty—her tranquility, compassion, and wisdom—are her real adornments. Her dazzling jeweled necklaces, armlets, anklets, earrings, and tiara indicate that the six far-reaching attitudes or *paramitas*—generosity, ethics, patience, joyous effort, concentration, and wisdom—are fully integrated in her being and decorate her every activity.

Tara is also adorned with three syllables: OM at her crown chakra, AH at her throat chakra, and HUM at her heart chakra. These three syllables embody respectively, a Buddha's physical, verbal, and mental faculties. They also represent respectively the Sangha, Dharma, and Buddha Jewels of refuge. These syllables serve as subtle objects upon which a meditator may focus; they also remind us of the qualities we are developing within ourselves as a result of practicing the Buddha's teaching. In this way, each characteristic of Tara's form illustrates the path to Buddhahood and its resultant qualities.

TARA AS THE RESULTANT BUDDHA

A third way to view Tara is as the reflection of our present Buddha-potential in its future fully developed state. How do we attain Buddhahood? In brief, we follow a path in which we generate: first, the determination to be free from cyclic existence; second, the altruistic intention (*bodhichitta*); and third, the correct view, the wisdom realizing emptiness. These three will be explained in future chapters, and the wisdom realizing emptiness, which is Tara's and our own ultimate nature, will be elaborated upon in chapters 9 and 10.

Our extremely subtle mind and body have the potential to transform into the fully enlightened body and mind of a Buddha. When we visualize Tara and regard her as the resultant Tara that we will become, we are inspired to train our mind in the path leading to this result. Let's examine how the practice of Tara does this.

Meditating on Tara

A Tara *sadhana*—a text of a guided meditation on Tara—is followed in order to purify our mind and cultivate our qualities so that we can become Tara. What follows is a general explanation of the outline of the important points contained in many Tara sadhanas. To do the Tara practice, certain requirements are necessary. Practitioners should consult a qualified teacher of Tibetan Buddhism. The following description alone is not to be used for meditation.

A sadhana begins with visualizing Tara and seeing her as the embodiment of the Three Jewels: Buddha, Dharma, and Sangha. Then we take refuge in the Three Jewels and generate the altruistic intention of bodhichitta. Contemplating these, we clarify our spiritual direction and our motivation for following it.

Visualizing Tara and contemplating the symbolisms of her body help us to cultivate respect for virtuous qualities and inspire us to develop those qualities ourselves. The purpose of doing the Tara practice is not to worship Tara. Tara is a fully enlightened Buddha; she doesn't need our worship or offerings. We don't do these practices for the sake of the enlightened beings, to win their favor or soothe their wrath. As a Buddha, Tara is free from ego needs and only experiences infinite bliss. Rather, bowing, making offerings, reciting mantra, and so on generate special feelings within our own mind. We do these practices in order to transform our attitude so that we can develop the same enlightened qualities as Tara.

The purpose of meditating on Tara isn't to feel good by worshiping an external deity, "I offered apples to Tara, so I'm happy because now she'll help me." The ultimate purpose of showing respect and praising Tara's qualities is to provoke us to contemplate: How can I develop those same qualities? How can I transform my mind to become more like Tara?

Seeing Tara with her right hand reaching out and her right foot extended to benefit others causes us to reflect: Do I reach out to benefit others? Do I approach others with openness? Or am I suspicious of them and need to check things out to see if I'm safe first? Her image acts as a mirror for us to examine ourselves and to contemplate how we can approach others with an open hand and kind heart. What attitudes and emotions do we need to develop so that we will have a more open attitude toward others and can approach them with more acceptance, respect, and affection? What are some small things that we can do in our lives that would indicate these attitudes and emotions? These questions lead us back into the Lamrim, the gradual path to enlightenment, which describes how to develop those excellent qualities.

How do we bridge the gap between a simple act of helping someone in our daily life and Tara's ability to make infinite manifestations throughout all universes? We must progress gradually and consistently. Our practice of the Dharma path resembles a child going to school. When we are in kindergarten, we do what kindergartners are capable of. When we're in first grade, we develop the skills of first graders. By the time we are in fifth grade, we have fifth grade abilities. In this way, we gradually advance as we go through school. If we don't do kindergarten and first and second grade, there's no way we reach high school and university.

Similarly, in learning the Dharma, we have to practice at our own level. At the beginning we are kindergarten Buddhists and that's okay. We see our older brothers and sisters who have already gotten their Ph.D.s, but they started out in kindergarten just like us. They are good examples for us because they show us what we can become when we practice with sincerity and perseverance.

A good spiritual mentor leads us skillfully so that our capabilities expand naturally. Once the Buddha encountered a person who suffered from extreme miserliness. The Buddha asked her to practice giving a carrot from her left hand to her right hand to become familiar with giving. I can identify with this lady, because sometimes my stinginess won't allow me to use the things I have. I want to have my cake and eat it, too, but if I have to choose, having it is more important because that gives me a sense of security. Cake is an example; we may enact this behavior in other aspects of our life. Generosity is the antidote that frees our mind.

At first, it's hard for us to give to others, so we give a carrot from one hand to the other. Then we give away simple things, such as a jar of thumbtacks. Then, we grow a little bit and give away things that we hold more dear. Later, we can share our time or whatever else is more difficult for us to give. When we eventually become Tara, we will be able to give everything effortlessly and joyfully.

Progressing gradually is important. We begin by giving to the people we care about, because that's not too difficult. Then, we practice giving to strangers, which is a little bit more difficult. As our confidence and joy in giving increase, we can practice giving to people we don't like. It's a gradual path and each step depends on the former ones.

As beginners, we need to rejoice in what we do well. Instead of saying, "Poor me, I'm so stingy; I'll never be like Tara," let's rejoice in the level of generosity we currently have and gradually expand it. For example, if we meet a five-year-old who laments that he isn't big enough to play with the first graders, we would say, "You're in kindergarten. That's wonderful. Enjoy your kindergarten friends. Next year you'll be in first grade, and you can play with the first graders then."

The Purpose of a Sadhana

Sadhanas, with their visualization practices and mantras, contain within them the entire meaning of the gradual path to enlightenment. I emphasize this because sometimes people meditate on deity just to feel good, without thinking about the meaning of the sadhana or using it to change their mind.

This may stem from a common misunderstanding among Westerners about Tibetan Buddhism. I have heard people speak of Theravada, Mahayana, and Vajrayana as if they were three distinct types of Buddhism, implying that those who practice Vajrayana do not do Theravada or Mahayana practices. Others think that if someone practices Mahayana, she doesn't practice Theravada teachings. Some Westerners believe that Tibetan Buddhism is only Vajrayana, that it doesn't include the Theravada or general Mahayana teachings. Such ideas are incorrect.

Tibetan teachers make it clear that someone following Tibetan Buddhism doesn't practice only Vajrayana. Visualizations and the chanting of mantras are not separate practices that are unrelated to other Buddhist practices. To do tantric practices, we have to be firmly grounded in the foundational teachings of the Theravada—the three higher trainings of ethical discipline, concentration, and wisdom. In addition, we must practice the general Mahayana path to develop bodhichitta and meditate on wisdom. Then, on the basis of all these practices, we take initiations and do tantric visualizations and meditations. If we understand foundational teachings and sadhana practice, we'll see that almost all of the foundational teachings are contained within a sadhana—refuge, the determination to be free, the four immeasurables, the three higher trainings, bodhichitta, and wisdom. If we don't understand this, we won't be able to properly meditate on the sadhana. However, when we understand this well, our practice becomes very rich and comprehensive.

Refuge

At the beginning of a sadhana, we go for refuge and generate bodhichitta. The process of going for refuge clarifies for us who our spiritual guides are, from whom we receive spiritual direction, and what our spiritual goal is. Without this clarity, sustaining a spiritual practice and plumbing its depths is difficult.

Generating the altruistic intention of bodhichitta enables us to know why we are pursuing this path. This, too, is important, because the result of our spiritual practice depends on the motivation with which we do it.

Going for refuge means entrusting our spiritual guidance to the Buddha, Dharma, and Sangha. That is, we have examined Buddhist teachings and are confident that they are accurate and that following them will lead to our desired goal: liberation or enlightenment. This is the meaning of becoming a Buddhist.

As followers of the Buddha's path, we should not criticize other religions or utter blanket statements of intolerance. The existence of many religions in the world is not only practical, but advantageous. Each religion is designed to help its followers cultivate ethical discipline and a kind heart. Therefore, anyone who sincerely practices the good teachings of their tradition will benefit and will contribute to well-being in the world. Since different explanations, symbolism, and practices benefit different people, the existence of a variety of spiritual paths enables each person to choose what suits him or her best.

Putting people in categories—"He is a Christian (Buddhist, Jew, Muslim, Hindu, or Wicca)"—and thinking that therefore we understand them is ignorant on our part. Not everyone who identifies themselves with a particular religion has the same views or practices in the same way. Christian mystics and born-again Christians may have very different views of who or what God is. Some people who consider themselves Buddhists may pray to Tara as if she were an external God, while some Christians may see God as emptiness or compassion.

Becoming enlightened doesn't depend on calling ourselves "Buddhist." It depends on what we believe in our heart and how we practice to transform our mind. Any person who generates the determination to be free from cyclic existence, the altruistic aspiration for enlightenment, and the wisdom realizing emptiness can become a bodhisattva and a Buddha. It doesn't matter what they call themselves. We have to look at what a person believes and practices in order to evaluate whether their realizations are correct realizations or not. For this, developing discriminating wisdom and open-mindedness are essential.

While religious tolerance is extremely important, it doesn't mean that all religions are the same or that all religions lead to the same result. We have no way of proving that they all bring the same result. We haven't completed even the Buddhist path, let alone the paths of other religions to be able to know with certainty whether these various paths lead to the same or different results.

In the 1990s, His Holiness the Dalai Lama and Father Lawrence Freeman, osb, an English Catholic priest who organized the John Main Seminar in which His Holiness spoke about the Gospels to Christian monastics, met in Bodhgaya, India, for interfaith dialogue. Father Lawrence brought a group of Christians to Bodhgaya, and some Buddhists attended the dialogue as well. Everyone practiced and discussed together. I heard from a friend who attended that Father Lawrence was in awe of His Holiness and repeatedly said that their two religions were very similar. At one point, His Holiness said, "No, there are differences. It's important to acknowledge the differences and not just make everything the same. Each faith has its own unique qualities, and we need to respect them for that."

When we say that all religions lead to the same place, it seems that we're trying to convince ourselves that underneath it all, those people actually believe what we believe so we don't need to distrust them. This kind of thought can make us feel that everything's okay. In the above story, His Holiness's comment emphasizes that religious harmony and tolerance do not depend on thinking that others' beliefs are the same as ours, only expressed with different words. Rather, we can acknowledge our different views—and even debate them—but still respect each other and get along. We appreciate that others' paths help them to become better people and rejoice that they practice the religion they do because that path, its symbolism, and its framework help them. If those people tried to use Buddhist symbols, they might not work for them. If they tried to adopt Buddhist views, they might become confused.

Before getting attached to calling ourselves "Buddhists" and boasting of the superiority of our path, we need to investigate, "Do my views actually correspond to what the Buddha taught?" We must look inside and investigate if we really hold Buddhist views. We may say that we're a Buddhist but not actually know or agree with what the Buddha taught. For example, some people say, "I'm Buddhist," but they don't want to hear teachings on the sutras spoken by the Buddha. They just want to receive blessings and initiations from high lamas. They think some external force or realized being will tap them on the head or give them blessed water and their life will go well. Some of them aren't interested in liberation or even in preparing for future lives. Do these people hold Buddhist views?

We need to look inside ourselves and see to what extent we are training our mind in Buddhist views. Such training doesn't mean we simply say, "Whatever the Buddha believed is right," and then blindly follow what other people tell us the Buddha said. Making loyalty statements to the Buddha is not a quality of a sincere practitioner. Rather, the Buddha wants us to listen to the teachings, think about them, meditate on them, and put them into practice. Through reflecting on their meaning, understanding them, and applying them to our own mind we'll come to understand how our mind functions. Thus, faith and confidence in the Buddhas, Dharma, and Sangha come from examination of the teachings and conviction that they show a viable path to enlightenment.

BODHICHITTA

Generating bodhichitta depends on having impartial love and compassion for all sentient beings. We ordinary beings see love as a limited commodity; it's a fixed pie and we feel we only have a limited amount. "If I give some to you, I can't give as much to others. And if I give it to everybody else, I can't give it to you." That kind of love has strings and conditions attached. It's a narrow and limited understanding of what love means; it's not the kind of love that Tara has. A Buddha's love remains constant. It is shared with everyone, no matter how they treat that Buddha. Tara's love and compassion do not depend upon whether other people like her or not, whether others praise her or not, whether they go along with her ideas or not.

But for us, whom do we love more, the people who praise us or the people who criticize us? The people who agree with our ideas or the people who don't? The people who do things our way or the people who don't? The people who give us things or the people who take them away? Whom do we love more?

Right away we see that our love is conditional. "As long as you're nice to me, I will love you." It's extremely easy to love somebody who's kind to us. Even cats do that. Animals love us if we're nice to them, pet them, and give them a treat. If we take away their food, they growl at us. We're similar. "If you give me something I like, I will love you; if you interfere with my happiness, I will hiss and growl." Loving somebody who's nice to us isn't a particularly human quality. If we want to do something more extraordinary as human beings, we must do a little better than this. When we practice cultivating the kind of love that Tara has, we try to free ourselves from having strings attached to our affection; we try to open our hearts impartially to all.

The strings we attach to our love are based on how somebody treats us. "I'll love you if you're nice to *me*. If you're nice to Osama bin Laden, I don't love you. In fact, I may even wish you harm." "If you're nice to *my* cats, I love you, but if you're nice to my friend Claire's cat, I don't care as much." Claire cares a lot about that and she'll love you if you care about her cat, but her cat isn't as important to *my self-centeredness*. The issue isn't whether you're nice to others or to cats in general; it's whether you're nice to *me* and to *my* cats.

It's interesting to look over past relationships to see how much self-centeredness has limited the love we've given to others. We ration out our very precious love only if someone is nice to *me*. "If you give me presents, if you praise me, if you comfort me when I'm down, I'll love you. But if you give presents to Charlie over there, I don't care—that is, unless Charlie is somehow related to *me*."

This concept of self and our self-centeredness get in the way of developing bodhichitta and opening our hearts to others. We evaluate and judge others in terms of how they relate to "*I, me, my, and mine*." It's extremely difficult for us to get beyond that. To loosen this, in our meditation we think, "How would I look at that person if I took the 'I' out of the picture? What would it be like if I stopped evaluating people in terms of my ideas and what they can do for me?"

Sometimes our mind resists practicing like this. We're so used to being in the picture that we don't even realize that we're there. But when we begin to take ourselves out, it feels terribly unnatural. For example, we might start our meditation session contemplating, "I'll take myself out of the picture. It doesn't matter if Harry gives me presents or is nice to me. I'm not going to judge or evaluate him based on his actions. I'll relate to him as if there were no 'me' in there." That's fine for a while. But then the mind observes, "Harry is a very caring person, but Sam is so selfish. Clearly, a caring person is more worthy of my love than a selfish one." Superficially, it looks like this evaluation has nothing to do with us. Is that true? Is the "I" totally out of the evaluation? No. Why not? I consider Harry kind because his actions accord with *my* definition of kindness. And Sam is a jerk, because he fits *my* definition of a jerk. I'm still evaluating people according to whether they fit into how I think things should be.

It's especially tricky when other people, such as our friends, agree with our definitions. Then we justify, "It's not just my definition of who's good and kind. This is everybody's definition of who is worthwhile. I'm looking at people objectively." But this is not necessarily the case. There are other people with different definitions of goodness and kindness.

In Buddhist practice, we try to develop a love for others that goes beyond how they superficially act or think. We cultivate a love that wants them to have happiness and its causes. Wanting sentient beings, including ourselves, to have happiness and its causes is the definition of love. Simply because a sentient being exists, we want him or her to be happy. Just because they are sentient beings who experience happiness and suffering, we want them to have happiness and be free from suffering. There are no other criteria for our love. It doesn't matter if they like us or not, agree with us or not, appreciate us or not, respect us or not. Our love is totally unconditional.

We habitually think that others have to earn our love, which means that they must correspond with our definition of right, good, accurate, and true. Our notion of punishment is similar: People who are bad are not worthy of our love and, in fact, deserve to be punished. And if we punish them and make them miserable enough, they'll realize that we were right all along and they'll decide to be nice to us...and then we'll love them.

We have the subconscious belief: "If I make you miserable enough, eventually you'll change to be more like I want you to be and then I'll love you." Is it reasonable to expect someone to love us, or even to like us, if we treat them poorly? If we punish them? Flip the situation around: How do we react when people make us miserable? We resent them; we criticize and put them on trial in our minds. When somebody does something we don't like, first our mind arrests him: "You were rude to me. You're under arrest." Then, we become the prosecutor and prosecute him, displaying all our evidence to prove they are guilty: "You didn't invite me to this meeting. Then you put my name last on the list of credits. And you didn't respond to my email." We're also the judge and jury who convict them: "Guilty, as charged. Punishment: I will take every opportunity to discredit you to your face and behind your back." Of course, such a case is always decided in our favor. The verdict is that we were right and he's wrong. Case settled. We're always the victor and the other person is always a loser in these internal court cases.

Because we've condemned that person a loser, we think there's no reason to care about him. "He's a jerk; therefore, I should be mean to him. I should punish him and be rude to him." Or, if we're "practicing patience," instead of saying something nasty to him, we just ignore him. We easily react in this way. If somebody criticizes us or does something we don't like, we instantly attack. Even though we may not physically or verbally assault them, in our mind we indict and convict them. We may even succumb to what they want because we're afraid of them, but in our mind, we can't stand them.

Instead of going along with this knee-jerk reaction, we now slowly try to train our minds in Tara's love. We try to relax the instinctual response to hiss and growl at others. Instead, we train our minds and hearts to look at them with compassion, "This is a sentient being who wants happiness just like me and doesn't want suffering. That's all. She's acting that way because she's unhappy. She wants to be happy and mistakenly thinks that her actions will bring her happiness." In this way, we look into others' hearts and understand their experience. In other words, we take the "I" out of the picture and think, "How they're treating me is not the most important issue. What they're doing is not about me. It's about their pain." Can we look at Osama bin Laden and think this way? Can we see the colleague who criticizes us as an unhappy sentient being? Can we wish from our heart, "How wonderful it would be if he were happy and free from misery"?

Wishing others to be happy doesn't mean we give them everything they want, because sometimes what they want can be harmful. Wishing them to be happy entails wanting them to be free from pain and loneliness. Wouldn't it be wonderful if they were free from these and all other miseries?

In order to love others, we have to be able to overcome our anger and hatred toward them. We have to be able to forgive them for the wrongs they've done. To do that, we have to get "me" out of the way and see that when people create harm, it is a reflection of their own pain, confusion, and misery. We just happened to walk across their path. We may even have done something to antagonize them, either deliberately or accidentally, but the reason that they got so upset is because of what is going on inside of them. We might also look at how we made ourselves into a target or accidentally became a target onto which they projected their confusion. Maybe we weren't very considerate of them. Maybe we have certain bad habits of which we're not aware and to which they're reacting.

Here is a summary of some of the points to think about:

1. Think about the way in which our self-centeredness steps in and discriminates who is nice and who is mean, who is our friend and who is our enemy. Make specific examples in your life of that habit and observe how you judge and evaluate according to *me*.

2. Contemplate taking the "I" out of the equation and see if it's easier to feel affection or connection to others. Are your heart and mind more open? Notice if there are still subtle ways that the focus on "me" sneaks in.

3. Try taking the "I" out of relationships with those whom we're not getting along with or toward whom we feel hostile. Try to see their behavior as a manifestation of their own pain and confusion. Wish them to be happy and to be free of misery and bewilderment. Apply this to people in your life with whom you have problems, be they personal problems or global conflicts, and see if it's possible to soften your tough preconceptions a bit. Start out with someone for whom your hostility is mild, not the person you hate the most. Next, try it with another person whom you dislike more. Then go on to a person that you feel afraid of or threatened by, and think that way in relation to him or her. As you relax into a more loving state, let your mind/heart rest in the state of forgiveness. Let go of anger and let your mind be peaceful. If you are able to take the next step, imbue your mind with the loving feeling that wants them to be happy.

Meditating on Tara

Next in the sadhana, we purify negativities and create positive potential through practicing the seven-limb prayer. The first limb, prostration, purifies pride and cultivates respect for an enlightened one's magnificent qualities, thus opening ourselves to develop those qualities. The second limb, making offerings, involves offering both real and imagined beautiful objects. This purifies miserliness and cultivates delight in generosity. The third limb, revealing our mistaken actions, purifies denial, justification, rationalization, and other unhealthy psychological machinations that prevent us from being honest with ourselves. Revealing our errors cultivates honesty and humility. The fourth, rejoicing in our own and others' virtues, cuts jealousy and develops delight in the goodness and attainments of others. The fifth and sixth limbs, requesting the Buddhas and our spiritual mentors to remain in our world and to teach us the Dharma, purify any harm or disrespect we may have shown toward them and help us to appreciate their presence in our lives. The seventh limb, dedication, shares the positive potential from the above practices with all beings and dedicates it for their temporary and ultimate well-being.

The sadhana continues with verses praising Tara's qualities and requesting her inspiration for our spiritual practice. These verses, recited while we visualize Tara in front of us, focus our attention on her enlightened qualities. The more we reflect upon Tara's wonderful qualities, the more we will receive the happiness that comes from following the spiritual path she taught. These verses help us give voice to our noblest spiritual aspirations, and by doing so, we are energized to actualize them.

The heart of the sadhana—the dissolution into emptiness and the self-generation—follows. Tara now comes on top of our head and dissolves into green light that flows into us and merges with our heart-mind in our heart chakra. At this point we meditate on selflessness, the emptiness or lack of independent or inherent existence. That is, there is no solid "me" meditating, no concrete Tara to meditate on, and no findable action of meditation. All false appearances of inherent existence cease and we rest our mind in the ultimate nature.

Within this empty space that is free from all false, dualistic appearances, our wisdom appears in the form of Tara, whose body is made of radiant green light. Still aware of the absence of an independently existing "I," we simultaneously label "I" in dependence on the appearance of Tara's body and mind. Having neither a solid conception of self nor the self-centeredness that it engenders, we nevertheless have the sense of being Tara and envision performing her enlightening activities to benefit all beings. We imagine feeling the impartial love and compassion for all beings that Tara feels and having her skillful means to be able to benefit them. From our Tara body made of light, we emanate countless small Taras that radiate throughout the universe, touching each sentient being, alleviating their suffering and becoming what they need. All sentient beings' defilements are purified and they gain Tara's realizations. Now that all beings have become Tara, we make offerings to them. These offerings generate in their minds bliss uncontaminated by attachment. Then all these Taras fall like snowflakes into us, blessing and inspiring our mind.

Like a child who dresses up and pretends to be a fireman, thereby developing the confidence to become one, we imagine ourselves to be a Buddha who relates to people as a fully enlightened being does—without ignorance, hostility, or clinging attachment and with immeasurable wisdom, compassion, and skill. In this way, we train our mind to think and act like a Buddha by bringing the Tara we will become in the future into the present moment and imagining being that Tara. This plants the seeds for us to actually become Tara in the future. Identifying ourselves with our Tara-nature, we gain invigorating confidence that spurs us to make our life meaningful.

TARA'S MANTRA

The visualization of performing Tara's enlightening activities is often done while reciting her mantra, OM TARE TUTTARE TURE SOHA. A mantra is a set of Sanskrit syllables uttered by a Buddha when in deep meditative equipoise on the nature of reality. We recite a mantra in order to calm our energies, concentrate our mind, and approach a state of meditative equipoise. In Green Tara's mantra, OM represents Tara's body, speech, and mind, the faculties that we want to develop. TARE, TUTTARE, and TURE all have the meaning of "to liberate." In one interpretation, these liberate us from the obstacles to generating the paths of the three levels of practitioner—initial, intermediate, and advanced. An initial practitioner wants to avoid unfortunate rebirths and thus takes refuge in the Three Jewels and observes karmic cause and effect in order to secure a fortunate rebirth. An intermediate practitioner is determined to be free from all sufferings of cyclic existence and to attain liberation. She practices mainly the three higher trainings—ethics, concentration, and wisdom—as the path to liberation. An advanced practitioner wishes all sentient beings to be free from cyclic existence and aims for full enlightenment in order to guide them to nirvana, and thus generates bodhichitta—the aspiration to attain enlightenment for the benefit of all sentient beings. She then practices the six far-reaching attitudes as well as the tantric path as the method to attain enlightenment. By actualizing these three levels of the path, our body, speech, and mind are purified, and we attain Tara's body, speech, and mind.

In another interpretation, TARE, TUTTARE, and TURE banish the obstructions to generating the three principal aspects of the path—the determination to be free, the altruistic intention of bodhichitta, and the wisdom realizing emptiness. The determination to be free is also called renunciation. It is a state of mind in which we have seen the defects of cyclic existence, and with compassion for ourselves, we seek a state of lasting happiness that is founded on wisdom, not the vagaries of transient sense objects. Based on compassion for all sentient beings, the altruistic intention, or bodhichitta, inspires us to seek full enlightenment, the total purification of mind and complete development of our positive qualities and potentials. The wisdom realizing emptiness penetrates into the deeper mode of existence of all persons and phenomena. As the direct antidote to the ignorance which misapprehends the nature of reality, this wisdom is what actually purifies our mind.

In a third way of interpretation, TARE means liberating from cyclic existence, that is, from uncontrolled, repetitive rebirth with a body and mind under the influence of ignorance. Of the Four Noble Truths, TARE liberates from the first Noble Truth, true suffering. TUTTARE indicates liberation from the eight dangers, various disturbing emotions that will be discussed below. Thus, TUTTARE liberates us from the second Noble Truth, true origins of suffering—afflicted attitudes and emotions, and the contaminated actions they motivate. TURE liberates from disease. Since the most severe disease from which we suffer is the afflicted attitudes and emotions and the subtle obscurations on the mind, TURE indicates the third Noble Truth—true cessation of suffering and its origins. Such liberation is our ultimate purpose and is actual spiritual success. This is arrived at through practicing the fourth Noble Truth, the path to enlightenment. SOHA means, "May this come about." It indicates planting the root of the path to full enlightenment in our hearts.

A praise to Tara's mantra illustrates the qualities of each syllable group:

> OM to the transcendent subduer, Arya Tara, I prostrate.
> Homage to the glorious one who frees with TARE;
> With TUTTARA you calm all fears;
> You bestow all success with TURE;
> To the sound SOHA I pay great homage.

Briefly, this is the way that the Tara sadhana guides our mind on the path to full enlightenment. As practitioners progress and generate an altruistic intention, single-pointed concentration, and insight into the nature of reality, their spiritual mentor will instruct them in more advanced visualizations and meditations to purify their extremely subtle body and mind. By means of these meditations, they will be able to work in wondrous ways to benefit all beings.

3

Tara, Liberator
from the Eight Dangers

THE EIGHT DANGERS

IN THE PREVIOUS CHAPTER, we noted that the syllable TUTTARE in Tara's mantra indicates that Tara liberates us from eight external and eight internal dangers. While the eight external ones threaten our life or property, the eight internal ones endanger us spiritually by turning us away from the path to enlightenment. Each external danger is coupled with an internal disturbing attitude or emotion: the lion of pride, the elephant of ignorance, the fire of anger, the snakes of jealousy, the thieves of wrong views, the chains of miserliness, the flood of attachment, and the carnivorous demon of doubt.

In some translations, these are called the eight fears. However, because "fear" is an easily misunderstood word, I prefer "danger." In the West, when we say "fear," worry, panic, and terror come to mind. However, Buddhism discriminates two types of fear, one that is defiled, the other that is a form of wisdom. The defiled fear is emotional terror and panic. This mental state is a hindrance on the path because it prevents us from thinking clearly. "Wise fear," on the other hand, is an awareness of danger that is helpful to have. It propels us to think creatively about how to deal with a possibly adverse situation. For example, parents educate their children to have a wise fear of matches. They want their children to respect the power of fire without becoming so terrified that they cry when seeing a match being lit. When we merge into traffic on a highway, we have a wise fear of possible danger. In neither of these cases is a person so terrified that he is immobilized by emotional fear and acts erratically.

How does Tara protect us from danger? The real protection is the Dharma Jewel in which we take refuge—the true paths and true cessations of sufferings and their origins in our mindstream. To cultivate and then perfect these paths and cessations, we must first learn about them, then reflect on their meaning, and finally familiarize ourselves with them in meditation and in daily life. To accomplish these three steps, depending on a qualified spiritual teacher is essential.

It is in this way that Tara frees our mind. First she teaches us the Dharma, and then she stimulates us to investigate its meaning so that we reach a correct understanding. Finally, she guides us in meditation practice so that we generate transformative realizations rather than mere fantastic experiences. Enlightened beings cannot take our defilements away like pulling a thorn from someone's foot. Nor can they give us their realizations like pouring water into an empty bowl. Rather, the help they give is by teachings us the path to enlightenment, the Dharma.

Another way of seeing how Tara liberates us is to recall that she is the wisdom of bliss and emptiness. She is all the realizations of the path. These realizations are what save us from danger and liberate us. Thus, when we say, "Please protect us from this danger!" we do not expect a green goddess to swoop down from the sky and rescue us by taking us to another place. Rather, we are calling out to our own wisdom, invoking our own understanding of the path so that it can protect us from the dangers of disturbing emotions.

The following eloquent verses requesting Tara to protect us from the eight dangers are extracted from "A Crown Ornament for the Wise," a hymn to Tara.[1] It was composed by Gyalwa Gendun Drubpa, the First Dalai Lama (1391–1475) after he completed a meditation retreat on Tara. These verses point out mental and emotional obstacles in the path so that we will investigate and understand how they operate in our mind. Then we can apply the

---

1. Based on translations by Martin Willson and Glenn Mullin.

antidotes that the Buddha taught first to subdue and finally to eradicate them so that they never reappear in our mind.

The Lion of Pride

> Dwelling in the mountains of wrong views of selfhood,
> Puffed up with holding itself superior,
> It claws other beings with contempt:
> The lion of pride—please protect us from this danger!

As spiritual practitioners, one of the greatest dangers we face is pride. Many damaging scandals involving spiritual practitioners have been unearthed in recent years, and in many of these, someone arrogantly thought he had reached a level of attainment that in fact he had not and then engaged in unethical actions. In other situations, a person considers themselves to be a competent teacher for subjects that they do not know well and by instructing others, they pass on their misconceptions to the students.

Just as a lion struts in mountain forests, our pride dwells in the environment of wrong views about the nature of the "I" or "self." Whereas the "I" is dependent, we grasp at it as existing independent of all other factors. This wrong view is the root of our suffering in cyclic existence.

Holding an unrealistic view of how we exist, we then compare ourselves with others. We become puffed up and proud over those who we deem inferior, jealous of those we consider superior, and competitive with equals. Our pride begets contempt that is like a lion's claws with which we injure other living beings. These harmful actions perpetuate our rebirth in unfortunate states of existence. Meanwhile, pride itself prevents us from recognizing our horrible predicament in cyclic existence because we arrogantly think we are flawless. Thus, we fail to practice the Dharma and consequently develop no new good qualities while the ones we have deteriorate.

Although a prideful person may consider himself outstanding, in fact, he may be foolish. Tibetans tell a story about an intelligent rabbit who got the better of an arrogant lion. On the full moon, the rabbit visited the lion and told him of a creature who was much more magnificent than he. Thinking this could not be the case, the lion immediately wanted to confront this creature. The rabbit brought the lion to a well and told him to look down. Upon seeing his own reflection, the lion began to show off his magnificence and strength. The being in the well did the same. Then the lion growled angrily, and the being in the well returned the threat. Determined to get the better of this creature, the lion pounced on his own reflection. Needless to say, he drowned in the well. We see many examples of arrogant politicians and CEOs who similarly destroy their lives.

The wisdom realizing the emptiness of inherent existence is the ultimate antidote to all eight inner fears, for it sees the true nature of the self—that it is empty of any permanent, independent, or inherent existence. However, since this realization takes time to generate and is difficult to gain, we use easier antidotes in the meantime. These "temporary" antidotes correspond to each particular affliction. In the case of pride, one such antidote is contemplation of a difficult topic, such as the twelve sources and eighteen elements. "What are those?" we may ask. But that is the point: these topics, while essential for actualizing the path, are difficult to understand. Recognizing how limited our current understanding is decreases our pride and makes us more humble.

Another antidote to pride is reflecting that everything we know and every talent and ability we have comes from the kindness of others. If we are a good athlete, we have our parents and coaches to thank. Our artistic or musical talent blossomed due to our teachers who cultivated it. Even something we take for granted, such as the ability to read, comes through the kindness and efforts of our teachers and those who wrote and printed books. Seeing this, how can we be proud, thinking that we have good qualities because we are someone special?

Bowing to the Three Jewels also helps to counteract arrogance, and for that reason, Tibetan Buddhist practitioners are encouraged to do 100,000 full-length prostrations. While prostrating, we contemplate the good qualities of the Buddha, Dharma, and Sangha, which makes respect and admiration arise in our mind. This reduces any embellishment we may have regarding our own qualities and inspires us to put energy into our spiritual practice so that we may emulate the Three Jewels. Physically lying on the ground with our face on the floor induces the feeling of humility and the relinquishing of ego.

Letting go of arrogance is a relief. Tremendous energy is required to try to convince ourselves and others that we are better than we are. When we free up and redirect that energy into taming our minds, our good qualities multiply quickly. In addition, our heart becomes lighter, we are able to laugh at our foibles, and we are no longer fearful of others "finding us out."

In asking Tara to save us from the danger of the lion of pride, we are actually calling upon our inner Tara—the seeds of our own wisdom and compassion. As these qualities gradually grow, they protect us from the damage that pride can inflict upon ourselves and others.

The Elephant of Ignorance

> Not tamed by the sharp hooks of mindfulness and vigilance,
> Dulled by the maddening liquor of sensual pleasures,
> It enters wrong paths and shows its harmful tusks:
> The elephant of ignorance—please protect us from this danger!

Powerful, yet out of control, a mad elephant terrorizes all in its path. It destroys crops cultivated with much care and endangers the lives of many. Similarly, uncontrolled emotions, which stem from ignorance, lead us to become involved in many unethical actions in our daily life. When we sit down to meditate, our mind is unable to focus and runs crazily from one object to another. This occurs because the ignorant mind has not been subdued by mindfulness and vigilance, mental factors that hook it so it remains focused on what is important. In the context of ethical behavior, mindfulness is aware of the guidelines within which we want to live, and vigilance checks us to see that we are living within them. In the context of meditation, mindfulness remembers the object of meditation so that our concentration can remain on it and is not distracted to another object. Vigilance investigates whether our mindfulness is active, or whether distraction or dullness has set in, interfering with our meditation.

When our mind is intoxicated by ignorant attachment to sense pleasures, we do whatever is necessary to procure the pleasure or advantage we seek, even if this entails piercing others with our tusks of flagrant harm. In addition, ignorance takes us down wrong paths that lead us to more confusion and suffering instead of to enlightenment.

When petitioning Tara for protection, we are calling forth our own powers of mindfulness and vigilance. Like a wise elephant tamer who skillfully knows how to subdue a wild elephant and harness its energy for constructive purposes, these two mental factors lead us to a non-violent lifestyle and to deep concentration. Mindfulness is developed by repeatedly recalling our ethical guidelines and our meditation object, and vigilance arises from frequently observing, "What is my mind focused on? What is going on in my mind?" When our mind is focused on something conducive to the path, vigilance lets it be. If we are distracted to sense pleasures, preoccupied with worries, or burning with anger, vigilance calls forth the appropriate antidote to calm whatever ignorant emotion plagues us at that moment.

The Fire of Anger

> Driven by the wind of inappropriate attention,
> Billowing forth swirling smoke-clouds of misconduct,
> It has the power to burn down forests of goodness:
> The fire of anger—please protect us from this danger!

Anger is compared to fire because of its power to destroy quickly and indiscriminately the positive potential, harmony, and trust among people that have been cultivated with great effort over a long period of time. Like a raging forest fire, anger begins with a tiny spark and, fueled by the wind of inappropriate attention that focuses on and exaggerates the negative qualities of someone or something, anger flares up. Blazing, it produces tumult in our own and others' lives by leading us into cloudy misconduct. Amidst the obscuring smoke of our harmful actions, we cannot see the source of our difficulties, and thus we do nothing to extinguish the fire of anger.

Under the influence of hatred and rage, we harm ourselves as well as others. As Dharma practitioners, we have tried to engage in constructive actions that leave positive karmic "seeds" on our mindstream. These seeds will produce happiness in our lives as well as enrich our mind so that crops of spiritual realizations will grow. However, anger burns these positive imprints, rendering them impotent. Thus, anger scorches not only the victim of our destructive deeds—another living being—but also the perpetrator—ourselves.

Patience, the ability to remain internally calm when confronting harm or suffering, is the antidote to anger. Patience does not mean passively giving in or foolishly condoning harm. Rather, it produces a certain mental stability so that our compassion and open-mindedness remain steady. Patience calms our mind so that with clarity and wisdom we can consider various courses of action and choose one that will bring the most benefit and least harm to everyone in the situation. With patience, we are able to act firmly—sometimes with peaceful strength, other times with assertive compassion.

The Snake of Jealousy

> Lurking in its dark pit of ignorance,
> Unable to bear the wealth and excellence of others,
> It swiftly injects them with its cruel poison:
> The snake of jealousy—please protect us from this danger!

Jealousy, like other disturbing emotions, stems from ignorance of the nature of reality. Jealousy ignorantly makes us think we'll be happy if we destroy others' happiness. Like a vicious snake whose venom kills a healthy person, jealousy poisons the happiness and goodness of both ourselves and others. While we say, "Love thy neighbor as thyself" and "May all beings be happy," when someone else has good fortune that we don't—even if we didn't have to lift a finger to bring about their happiness—our jealousy cannot endure their prosperity, ability, or virtue.

Overcome by jealousy we try to demolish others' happiness and success. Such behavior is self-defeating, because even if we succeed, we do not feel good about ourselves when we undermine others' well-being. Spiteful jealousy not only lessens our own self-respect; it also keeps us bound in pain. Like a snake killing its victim by constriction, jealousy wrings the life out of our mental peace. Sometimes only the pain of the jealousy itself stimulates us to seek out its antidote.

Rejoicing in the happiness, talents, fortune, and good qualities of others is that antidote. When others are happy, we might as well join in! When others act wisely and kindly, why not rejoice in their virtue? There is so much suffering in our world that to wish others to be deprived of the happiness they have is foolish.

Rejoicing is regarded as the lazy person's way to create great positive potential. When we rejoice at others' virtues—their kindness, generosity, ethical discipline, patience, joyous effort, concentration, wisdom, and so forth—we accumulate positive potential as if we had that admirable attitude or had done that beneficial action ourselves. Since we need to accumulate great positive potential to progress along the path, rejoicing at others' goodness and happiness is definitely worthwhile. It spurs us along the path to enlightenment and also makes us happy right now.

The Thieves of Distorted Views

> Roaming the fearful wilds of inferior practice
> And the barren wastes of absolutism and nihilism,
> They sack the towns and hermitages of benefit and bliss:
> The thieves of wrong views—please protect us from this danger!

When we have treasured possessions that bring us prosperity and joy, we diligently protect them from thieves. Similarly, we must take care that our accurate views on important spiritual matters are safeguarded, because these are the foundation of our spiritual prosperity. Should we follow distorted views, we will engage in practices that purportedly lead to enlightenment but actually do not. Thus, we will be left impoverished, stranded in a spiritual desert. Spiritual poverty is more dangerous than material poverty, for it affects not just the happiness of this life but the happiness of many future lives as well.

We might be surprised to discover the number of distorted views we hold and the stubborn tenacity with which we hold them. When someone challenges our distorted views, we become upset and defensive. We may even disparage the Buddha and the Dharma teachings when they don't agree with our opinions or our likes and dislikes. This is very harmful to our spiritual development.

Some people weave the Dharma into their own preconceived ideas in such a way that it seems the Dharma agrees with their opinions when in fact it does not. An example is using the Dharma to "prove" certain political views, when in fact the teachings either don't say anything about that issue or disagree with it. For example, the Buddha would not support assisted suicide. Saying that the Buddha taught us to be open-minded and that therefore assisted suicide is fine is not correct. Similarly, it is not suitable to use the teaching that a bodhisattva may stop people who are harming others by whatever means possible to justify bombing a country whose government one considers dangerous.

We may have a subconscious tendency to believe that the Buddha would agree with our political and social views, but this is our self-centeredness manifesting. We need to study the teachings carefully with an open mind to understand them and to apply them to situations around us in an unbiased way. We should not insist that everyone who "really understands the Dharma" holds the same political and social views that we do.

The thieves of distorted views are of many varieties. Some distorted views believe that unethical actions are ethical and that misconstrued practices lead to enlightenment. Distortion of religious teachings, such as thinking that killing infidels leads to rebirth in heaven, creates horror both in society and within those who hold such views.

The chief distorted views, like barren wastes in which no liberating activities grow, hold to the two extremes: absolutism and nihilism. The former reifies the way in which phenomena exist, while the latter negates their existence all together. While all persons and phenomena are empty of independent existence, absolutism holds that they exist independently. It sees phenomena as possessing their own inherent essence and existing under their own power, whereas they do not. Nihilism goes to the other extreme, believing that persons and phenomena do not exist at all. It disparages the functioning of cause and effect, thus destroying our respect for ethical living and making us reckless in practicing constructive deeds and abandoning harmful ones. When absolutism or nihilism is present, we are unable to understand properly either the ultimate nature or the conventional nature of phenomena.

The Middle Way view is the balance that is needed. It negates all fantasized ways of existence, including independent existence, but affirms that all persons and phenomena do exist on a conventional level. That is, although everything lacks independent existence, it exists dependently. Persons and phenomena are not solid things with their own immutable and inherent essence. Rather, they exist like illusions in that they appear one way but exist in another. That is, things appear to us as existing independently but this appearance is false, for in fact they exist in dependence on other factors. The Middle Way view enables us to distinguish accurately between what exists and what doesn't and between what to practice and what to abandon. In this way, our collections of wisdom and positive potential—which resemble towns and hermitages of ease and bliss—are protected, and our happiness ensured.

The Chain of Miserliness

> Binding embodied beings in the unbearable prison
> Of cyclic existence with no freedom,
> It locks them in craving's tight embrace:
> The chain of miserliness—please protect us from this danger!

Although ignorance is the root of cyclic existence, what keeps us locked in the cycle of suffering from one lifetime to the next is craving. In cahoots with craving is miserliness, the mind that clings to our possessions and can't bear to part with them. While we like to think of ourselves as generous people, when we examine our behavior, we find much room for improvement. For example, our closets and basements may be filled with things we don't use—in fact, we may not even remember having some possessions—but should we begin to clean out our storage areas, our mind concocts many reasons not to give these things away, even to people who clearly need them. "I may need it later," "This has sentimental value," "The people I give it to will take advantage of me and ask for more," "I don't want to appear as if I'm showing off by being generous," and on and on.

It's easy to think we're generous and magnanimous people when we're sitting here reading. We think, "I'm not attached. I'd be happy to share whatever I have with others." But should somebody ask us, "May I have the food in your cupboards?" we would probably respond, "No! Why should I give it to you?" Or if somebody took our shoes that we left outside the meditation hall, we would be upset. "Who took *my* shoes? How dare they! I want them back!"

Fear often lies behind our excuses. We falsely believe that possessions will bring us security in cyclic existence. In fact, our attachment to them keeps us bound in a prison of dissatisfaction. We constantly crave more and better, yet are never satisfied with what we have.

Stinginess is painful. When it arises in our mind, we are locked in its tight embrace; it imprisons us. When we recognize the faults of miserliness, we will have the courage to let it go because we want to be happy. Miserliness impedes our spiritual progress, turns us into hypocrites, and perpetuates our dissatisfaction. Starkly seeing this, we will want to apply the antidotes to it. For example, since we know how harmful a thief can be, when one enters our house, we don't ask him to sit down and have a cup of tea. In the same way, when we know the harm of disturbing emotions, we don't invite them into our mind and cater to them.

Non-clinging and generosity are the antidotes to miserliness. With non-clinging we don't conceive of material possessions as a reliable source of happiness or as the meaning of success. More balanced within ourselves, we discover contentment, a rare "commodity" in our materialistic society. Contentment allows us to cultivate the love that wishes others to have happiness and its causes, and thus we take delight in giving.

Giving with an open heart brings us joy and directly benefits others. Goods are then shared more equitably within our society and among nations, soothing the ill-feeling of social inequity and promoting world peace. Sharing is a source of our continued existence as a species. As His Holiness that Dalai Lama says, it is not survival of the fittest, but survival of those who cooperate the most, that makes a species prosper. None of us exists independently;

we have to depend on others simply to stay alive. Thus, helping others and sharing wealth benefits both self and others. Generosity makes us happy now, enables our species to continue to prosper, and creates positive karma that brings us prosperity in the future. In addition, it is an essential trait of an enlightened being. Who ever heard of a stingy Buddha?

The Flood of Attachment

> Sweeping us in the torrent of cyclic existence so hard to cross
> Where, conditioned by the propelling winds of karma,
> We are tossed in the waves of birth, aging, sickness, and death:
> The flood of attachment—please protect us from this danger!

Like a flood, attachment sweeps over us, propelling us helplessly in the stormy ocean of cyclic existence. It does this in two ways. First, under the influence of attachment—which clings to persons, objects, places, ideas, views, and so forth—we act in harmful ways in order to get what we want. Our destructive actions create conflict with others now and leave imprints on our mindstream that produce suffering situations later. Second, at the time of death, attachment arises once more, and we cling to our body and life. When we realize we cannot hold on to them any longer, attachment then grasps another body and life, and we are reborn in cyclic existence.

Attachment resembles a flood; we are powerlessly swept along by its current. When our mind is attached to something, it has no space for anything else. We are obsessed with the object of our attachment; we worry about not getting it and fear losing it once we do. Drowning in the flood of attachment, we cannot breathe the fresh air of satisfaction and peace. We may want to get to dry land, but not seeing a life raft, we continue to be swept along uncontrollably. The Dharma is our life raft. Let's make sure we hold on to it and not let it float past us.

Examining our patterns of attachment is very beneficial. If we find ourselves in similar situations or face similar problems again and again, we may want to investigate what we're clinging to: What do we think will make us happy? For example, some people get into one relationship after another, experiencing similar relationship problems each time. Their mind is seeking something that they aren't aware of; their mind is attached to something that cannot bring the happiness they seek.

In each rebirth, aging begins immediately after we are born, sickness occurs repeatedly, and death is their inevitable outcome. In the meantime, still swept along by the flood of attachment, we continue to act destructively, leaving more negative karmic imprints on our mindstream that cause yet more rebirths as we flounder in confusion and unhappiness.

Crossing the torrents of cyclic existence is not easy. We need a guiding star to find our way across the dark seas of the disturbing emotions. The Sanskrit noun *tara* means "star," and the verb *trri* indicates "to guide across, to cross over." We ask Tara to protect us from danger by teaching us the path to enlightenment. In this way she liberates us from cyclic existence and enables us to cross over to the other shore and arrive at a state of mental bliss and freedom.

Contemplating the transient nature of things is an excellent antidote to attachment. Seeing that the objects to which we cling change moment by moment, we know that they will not last long and thus are not reliable sources of happiness. Turning away from their deceptive lure, we have more time to focus on transforming our disturbing attitudes and emotions and developing beneficial ones. Through familiarizing our mind with the compassionate motivation of bodhichitta and the wisdom realizing emptiness, we progress through the stages of the bodhisattva path to Buddhahood.

Reflecting on the disadvantages of cyclic existence is another antidote. If a prisoner thinks that being in prison isn't too bad, he will have no interest in freeing himself from its confines. Similarly, as long as we believe cyclic existence—the process of being born repeatedly under the influence of ignorance, attachment, and hostility—to be comfortable, we won't seek liberation. For this reason, the Buddha, in his teaching on the Four Noble Truths, asked us first to reflect on the unsatisfactory nature of our existence and its causes so that we will seek their cessation and the path to that state of peace. We are born, age, become ill, and die without choice. We try hard to procure what is pleasing but aren't always successful. Sometimes we succeed, but then we are left disillusioned or are plagued by more problems. Meanwhile, difficulties, which we try so hard to avoid, readily befall us. Recognizing that this situation is unsatisfactory, we will seek to be free from it and will eagerly practice the path leading to true happiness.

The Carnivorous Demon of Doubt

> Roaming in the space of darkest confusion,
> Tormenting those who strive for ultimate aims,
> It is viciously lethal to liberation:
> The carnivorous demon of doubt—please protect us from
>   this danger!

Doubt is of various types, not all of them obstructive. The doubt that is curious and open-minded propels us to learn, examine, and clarify the meaning of a teaching. It aids us on the path. However, when our doubt dwells in confusion and leans toward distorted views, our mind spirals in circles of its own making and we are spiritually immobilized. This deluded doubt devours our time, squandering our chance for liberation. It resembles a carnivorous demon that destroys life, cutting short the blossoming of a person's potential.

Such skeptical doubt attacks us, "Why am I sitting here with my legs crossed and eyes closed? What kind of weird thing is Buddhism?" "Everybody at work thinks I'm nuts and tells me I should get a life." "Actually, cyclic existence isn't all that bad. Why should I want to get out of it?" "What's all this talk of helping all sentient beings? Benefit Osama bin Laden? Are you crazy? I don't want to help him! How can I have compassion for people who harm others?" All sorts of doubts pop up. We even get involved in doubting ourselves, "Dharma is too hard. I can't do it. Thinking I can overcome my self-centeredness is asking too much. Don't expect that much of me!" "Why is my teacher recommending that I do so many prostrations? Ridiculous! I might as well go to the gym for a work-out."

A mind spinning in doubt cannot go straight on the path to liberation. It is like trying to sew with a two-pointed needle; we can't go forward. If we start to do a practice, we doubt its efficacy and stop doing it. When we listen to teachings, we doubt their authenticity and stop listening. We doubt our ability to practice; we doubt the ability of our teacher to guide us; we doubt the path to practice; we doubt the existence of enlightenment. Unable to reach any resolution, we cannot go forward on the path, and our mind remains tormented. Our ultimate aims, liberation and enlightenment, are slaughtered by this demon of doubt.

To counteract doubt, we must first stop the flurry of contradictory thoughts and calm our mind. Meditation on the breath is an excellent way to dispel discursive thoughts and focus the mind. A settled mind can distinguish important issues that need consideration from skeptical, nonsensical thoughts.

Next, we must study the Buddha's teachings and learn to think logically and clearly so that we can investigate them and reach accurate conclusions. For this reason, Tibetan monastics spend years debating and discussing the scriptures. The formalized structure of debate teaches us how to examine the teachings clearly and test their validity. It also draws out deeper meanings of the teachings, shows us what we do and don't understand, and elucidates diverse perspectives. Although we may not engage in formal debate, discussing topics with Dharma friends serves the same purpose. In this way we can clarify what we believe, and having done that, we can begin to practice accordingly.

These are the eight dangers from which Tara protects us. In our meditation and in our life, let's be aware of when we are under the influence of these eight and investigate how they work. What are their causes? How do they function? What results do they bring? Then let's investigate how to counteract them and bring peace in our minds.

To release the eight dangers, we may do analytical meditation, contemplating their disadvantages and the antidotes to each as described above. We may also visualize Tara in front of us, radiating green light. This light flows into us, filling our body/mind, so that there is no space for the eight dangers or for the negative karma we have created under their influence. We may also imagine Tara's radiant green light filling the universe and all the beings within it, liberating them from the eight dangers and enhancing their love, compassion, and wisdom.

Dedication

> Through these praises and requests to you
> Quell conditions unfavorable for Dharma practice
> And let us have long life, positive potential, glory, plenty,
> And other conducive conditions as we wish!

By doing Tara practice and applying the antidotes to the eight dangers in order to benefit all beings, we have created tremendous positive potential. Directing how it will ripen, we now dedicate it for two principal purposes. The first is for all beings to be free from conditions that impede our practice and our integrating the Dharma in our minds. Such conditions may be external—such as war, poverty, excessive obligations, or lack of a qualified spiritual guide—or internal—such as disease, emotional turbulence, doubt, or mental incapacity.

Second, we dedicate our positive potential (merit) so that we and all others will meet conditions conducive for actualizing the path to enlightenment. Long life is important so that we are able to study and practice the Buddha's teachings for a long time. Positive potential enables us to die without regret and propels us toward fortunate rebirths in which we can continue our spiritual practice. It also fertilizes our mind so that we will understand the meaning of the Buddha's teachings easily and be able to integrate them into our lives. Material wealth provides us with necessities so we can practice without worry. It also allows us to share possessions with others, thus accumulating positive potential from generosity. Spiritual wealth enables us to meet a qualified spiritual mentor and good Dharma friends who encourage our practice. Glory can refer to the ability and conditions to help others skillfully. Plenty is the sense of richness that allows us to give our material possessions as well as to share our love, protection, and Dharma understanding with others in a skillful way.

Although the above verses are phrased in the manner of supplicating Tara to protect us from the various dangers, we must remember some important points in order to understand their meaning correctly. First, Tara is not a self-existent, independent deity or God. Like all persons and phenomena, she exists dependently and is empty of independent or absolute existence. We should avoid thinking of Tara as an external being who can wave a magic wand curing our difficulties and fulfilling our selfish desires while we sit back and relax. Instead, we make these requests with an awareness that we (the one making the request), Tara (the one we are requesting), and the action of requesting are all empty of independent existence, yet exist conventionally.

Second, although all beings who have become Tara are free from limitations from their side to help others, they are not omnipotent. They can teach, guide, and inspire us only to the extent that we are receptive. One of the purposes of reciting these and similar verses is to open our minds and hearts, making ourselves receptive spiritual vessels. Although we seem to be praying to Tara, we are invoking our internal wisdom and compassion through generating wonderful aspirations and directing our thought toward virtuous aims. The more we open our hearts with love and compassion to all beings equally, the more Tara can influence us. The greater our wisdom understanding the ultimate nature, the more Tara can inspire us to deepen our realizations.

"Homage to the Twenty-one Taras"

THE "HOMAGE TO THE TWENTY-ONE TARAS" is from the tantra *In Praise of Tara, the Mother of All Tathagatas.* Preceding the "Homage," it reads:

> Then the Bhagavan Buddha, a victorious, perfected, and transcendent lord, spoke to Manjughosha, the immortal bodhisattva of wisdom, "O Manjushri, the female form symbolizes the source of the Buddhas of the three times. Therefore, O Manjushri, as all the Buddhas of the past, present, and future sing this praise of her, you also should do so in your mind." Then the Bhagavan went on to speak the *dharani* in praise of Arya Tara.[2]

Written down in Sanskrit, the "Homage" was translated into Tibetan. The meaning of the verses is not clear from simply reading the "Homage," and a commentary is necessary to elucidate the meaning. Because various commentaries have different interpretations of phrases or verses, the translations into English will vary accordingly, as will the explanation of the meaning in Tibetan.

The following is a translation of the "Homage to the Twenty-one Taras" in a form that may be chanted in English.[3] Chanting the "Homage" out loud at a brisk speed gives us a lot of energy; contemplating its meaning increases

2. Translator unknown.
3. Translated from the Tibetan by Ven. Sangye Khadro and reprinted here with her permission.

our understanding, and visualizing the twenty-one Taras deepens our connection to them.

OM I prostrate to the noble, transcendent liberator.

1. Homage to Tara swift and fearless,
   With eyes like a flash of lightning,
   Lotus-born in an ocean of tears
   Of Chenresig, three worlds' protector.

2. Homage to you whose face is like
   One hundred autumn moons gathered
   And blazes with the dazzling light
   Of a thousand constellations.

3. Homage to you, born from a gold-blue lotus,
   Hands adorned with lotus flowers,
   Essence of giving, effort, and ethics,
   Patience, concentration, and wisdom.

4. Homage to you who crowns all Buddhas,
   Whose action subdues without limit;
   Attained to every perfection,
   On you the bodhisattvas rely.

5. Homage to you whose TUTTARA and HUM
   Fill the realms of desire, form, and space.
   You crush seven worlds beneath your feet
   And have power to call all forces.

6. Homage to you adored by Indra,
   Agni, Brahma, Vayu, and Ishvara,
   Praised in song by hosts of spirits,
   Zombies, scent-eaters, and yakshas.

7. Homage to you whose TREY and PEY
   Destroy external wheels of magic.
   Right leg drawn in and left extended,
   You blaze within a raging fire.

8. Homage to you whose TURE destroys
   The great fears, the mighty demons.
   With a wrathful frown on your lotus face,
   You slay all foes without exception.

9. Homage to you beautifully adorned
   By the Three Jewels' gesture at your heart.
   Your wheel shines in all directions
   With a whirling mass of light.

10. Homage to you, radiant and joyful,
    Whose crown emits a garland of light.
    You, by the laughter of TUTTARA,
    Conquer demons and lords of the world.

11. Homage to you with power to invoke
    The assembly of local protectors.
    With your fierce frown and vibrating hum,
    You bring freedom from all poverty.

12. Homage to you with crescent moon crown,
    All your adornments dazzling bright.
    From your hair-knot Amitabha
    Shines eternal with great beams of light.

13. Homage to you who dwells in a blazing wreath
    Like the fire at the end of this age.
    Your right leg outstretched and left drawn in,
    Joy surrounds you who defeats hosts of foes.

14. Homage to you whose foot stamps the earth
    And whose palm strikes the ground by your side.
    With a wrathful glance and the letter HUM
    You subdue all in the seven stages.

15. Homage to the blissful, virtuous, peaceful one,
    Object of practice, nirvana's peace.
    Perfectly endowed with SOHA and OM,
    Overcoming all the great evils.

16. Homage to you with joyous retinue,
    You subdue fully all enemies' forms.
    The ten-letter mantra adorns your heart,
    And your knowledge-HUM gives liberation.

17. Homage to TURE with stamping feet,
    Whose essence is the seed-letter HUM.
    You cause Meru, Mandara, and Vindhya,
    And all three worlds to tremble and shake.

18. Homage to you who holds in your hand
    A moon like a celestial lake.
    Saying TARA twice and the letter PEY,
    You dispel all poisons without exception.

19. Homage to you on whom the kings of gods,
    The gods themselves, and all spirits rely.
    Your armor radiates joy to all;
    You soothe conflicts and nightmares as well.

20. Homage to you whose eyes, the sun and moon,
    Radiate with pure brilliant light;
    Uttering HARA twice and TUTTARA
    Dispels extremely fearful plagues.

21. Homage to you, adorned with three natures,
Perfectly endowed with peaceful strength.
You destroy demons, zombies, and yakshas;
O ture, most exalted and sublime!

Thus, the root mantra is praised,
And twenty-one homages offered.

Commentary on "Homage to the Twenty-one Taras"

THE TWENTY-ONE TARAS have been described and drawn by various artists in different ways. Don't be surprised if the paintings you see are not all the same. Various commentaries may attribute different functions to a particular Tara than are highlighted in the verse. This does not mean that one commentary is correct and the others are not. Additional information can be found in Martin Willson's book *In Praise of Tara,* which contains more detail about the appearance of each Tara and the meaning of each word of the verses.

Please note that White Tara, whose specialty is long life, is not one of the twenty-one Taras. This enumeration of twenty-one Taras is not exhaustive. Another text speaks of 108 Taras!

The First Dalai Lama, Gendun Drub, outlined the "Homage" as follows.[4] The verses that pertain to each point of the outline are in parentheses. The word "homage" in this case means "praise," it also implies bowing and showing reverence.

1. Brief praise

2. Extensive praise
2.1 Praise of her story (1)

4. Based on the translation by Martin Willson.

2.2 Praise of her aspects (2–15)

2.2.1 Praise of her sambhogakaya aspect (2–14)
2.2.1.1 Praise of her peaceful aspects (2–7)
2.2.1.1.1 Praise of the brightness and luminosity of her face (2)
2.2.1.1.2 Praise of color, hand symbols, and causes (3)
2.2.1.1.3 Praise because she is honored by the Buddhas and bodhisattvas (4)
2.2.1.1.4 Praise for her suppression of adverse factors (5)
2.2.1.1.5 Praise because she is honored by the great worldly gods (6)
2.2.1.1.6 Praise because she destroys opponents (7)
2.2.1.2 Praise of her fierce aspects (8–14)
2.2.1.2.1 Praise of her subduing negative forces and cleansing the two obscurations (8)
2.2.1.2.2 Praise of her hand symbols (9)
2.2.1.2.3 Praise of her crown and laughter (10)
2.2.1.2.4 Praise of her accomplishing activities through the ten directional guardians (11)
2.2.1.2.5 Praise of her crown ornaments (12)
2.2.1.2.6 Praise of her fierce posture (13)
2.2.1.2.7 Praise of her HUM radiating light (14)

2.2.2 Praise of her dharmakaya aspect (15)

2.3 Praise of her activities (16–21)
2.3.1 Praise of her peaceful and fierce mantras (16)
2.3.2 Praise of her fierce activity of shaking the three worlds (17)
2.3.3 Praise of her dispelling poisons, animals, and so forth (18)
2.3.4 Praise of eliminating conflict and nightmares (19)
2.3.5 Praise of eradicating fever (20)
2.3.6 Praise of subduing evil spirits and zombies (21)

3. The benefits of praising the twenty-one Taras
3.1 Distinction of the thought
3.2 Distinction of the time

3.3 Actual explanation of the benefits

3.4 Condensed statement of the benefits in numerical terms

The outline and the explanations of the color and posture of a particular Tara may vary depending on which commentary we read.

The brief praise is OM *jetsunma pagma drolma la chag tsal lo* or "OM I prostrate to the Noble Transcendent Liberator." OM represents Tara's body, speech, and mind. Our goal is to transform our body, speech and mind so they become just like Tara's. *Jetsunma pagma drolma* means "noble transcendent liberator." This is Tara's name. She is an arya *(pagma)*, or noble one, because she has directly realized emptiness. She is *jetsunma*, which means "transcendent," indicating that she is the source of all Buddhas and that she keeps the three sets of vows—pratimoksha, bodhisattva, and tantric—purely. *Drolma* is the Tibetan name for Tara; it means "liberator." *La chag tsal lo* means "bow down," "prostrate," or "pay homage." Making this gesture of respect cleanses our mind of disturbing attitudes, negative emotions, and karma.

Paying homage or bowing is done physically, verbally, and mentally. Some people may physically bow down while reciting the "Homage," while others may visualize themselves surrounded by all sentient beings or by many replicas of their own body and imagine leading them in paying homage to Tara. Verbally, we recite the "Homage," and mentally our attitude is one of respect, admiration, and trust in Tara.

The following twenty-one verses are the extensive praise.

1. Homage to Tara swift and fearless,
   With eyes like a flash of lightning,
   Lotus-born in an ocean of tears
   Of Chenresig, three worlds' protector.

Tara Swift and Heroic is red in color. Her specific function is to control, and there is a ceremony in which a practitioner invokes this Tara to turn back the power of others. In other words, if others are trying to exert negative power over us, we can reverse that power or turn it away by requesting Tara's help.

Tara is swift because she is a female manifestation of the Buddha's omniscient mind. Feminine energy is said to be quick energy. Tara is swift to work for sentient beings. "Fearless" or "heroic" means that she is able to overcome all the demons—internal and external negative forces—before they arise. Internal demons are our afflictions: the disturbing attitudes and negative emotions. These can be stopped by the force of mindfulness and vigilance combined with wisdom.

External negative forces are forces or beings that interfere with our life or our Dharma practice. Various means can stop them. For example, when a wild elephant was charging at the Buddha, he meditated on love. By the power of his love for all beings, including the wild elephant, the elephant became tame and bowed to the Buddha. Different situations may require other skillful means to deflect negative energy or harmful beings. Some of these are gentle; others are assertive, firm, and stern.

"Eyes like a flash of lightning" means that Tara is able to see all of existence. Her eyes light up the world due to the power of her omniscient mind that simultaneously knows all existent phenomena. Omniscience gives her the power to benefit all sentient beings because she sees the specific karma they've created in the past and knows their particular dispositions and tendencies so she can teach them accordingly. That is a very important quality if we want to be able to benefit sentient beings. By knowing the karma they've created in the past, we will know with which teachers they have a karmic link, which path is most suitable for them, and what practices they have the disposition to practice. Because there are many Buddhist paths and teachings, to benefit others most effectively, we need to know exactly what to teach a person, when to teach her, and how to guide her in her practice. The more that we have a good motivation, purify our own mind, develop wisdom, and gain accurate clairvoyant powers, the more we will able to access this information and use it to benefit others.

Chenresig, from whose tear Tara was born, is called the "three worlds' protector." There are different ways of talking about the three worlds; here it refers to below, on, and above the earth. Below includes fish, other sea creatures, and hell beings. Those on the earth include human beings, animals, and hungry ghosts. Those above the earth are birds and various gods.

"Lotus-born in an ocean of tears of Chenresig, three worlds' protector" indicates the story of Tara's origin, which is why this verse is said to praise Tara's story. As a Buddha, Tara arose from perfected wisdom and compassion—that is, the two accumulations of wisdom and positive potential. Personally, I see the story which follows as a legend, but you may interpret it as you wish.

"Chenresig" is the Tibetan name for the Buddha of Compassion. Chenresig is revered in places where Mahayana Buddhism is practiced and is known by the names Avalokiteshvara (Sanskrit), Kuan Yin (Chinese), and Kannon or Kwannon (Japanese). In some places, Chenresig appears in a female form, and in others, in male form.

As the Buddha of Compassion, Chenresig put much effort into benefiting sentient beings. He worked and worked and worked and liberated countless sentient beings from cyclic existence. But every time he turned around, he saw so many more who were still suffering in cyclic existence. One time, he had liberated many beings from the hell realm, but when he looked again, the hell realm had filled up with many more sentient beings who had created the karma to be reborn in such extreme suffering. Although Chenresig had been trying so hard, the number of sentient beings in the hells wasn't decreasing significantly.

We can understand Chenresig's situation: He did so much and still there was more to do. Wondering if there would ever be an end to sentient beings' suffering, he became discouraged and began to cry. His tears formed a pool, and a lotus started to grow in the pool. The lotus opened up, and out came Tara who said, "Don't worry, I'll help you." Like a true Dharma friend, she encouraged him, "Don't be despondent. Don't get depressed. Just keep on going." That's why she's said to be lotus-born in an ocean of Chenresig's tears.

The story about Princess Yeshe Dawa in the first chapter and her vow to be enlightened in a female body is another story about Tara. Reflecting on both of these stories will inspire our practice.

Next is the section of praises of Tara's aspects, specifically her sambhogakaya (enjoyment body) aspect. In particular, verses 2 through 7 describe the peaceful sambhogakaya aspect.

2. Homage to you whose face is like
   One hundred autumn moons gathered

And blazes with the dazzling light
Of a thousand constellations.

This Tara is called Tara White as the Autumn Moon. Like a hundred luminous autumn moons, she is radiant white, indicating that she liberates sentient beings by peaceful methods and can pacify all their disturbing attitudes.
Four actions are often mentioned: (1) peaceful, (2) increasing, (3) influencing
or controlling, and (4) fierce or wrathful. Here, being white in color, Tara
shows the peaceful aspect, pacifying afflictions through peaceful means.

She is standing, and her specialty is pacifying infectious diseases. Here,
we're particularly praising her brightness and the luminous radiance of her
countenance, which comes from having practiced virtue for so long. When
someone cultivates a kind heart, her face lights up and the energy around her
changes.

3. Homage to you, born from a gold-blue lotus,
   Hands adorned with lotus flowers,
   Essence of giving, effort, and ethics,
   Patience, concentration, and wisdom.

This Tara is called Golden-Colored Tara, Giver of Supreme Virtue. She's gold
with a bluish hue, although some say she's blue with a golden hue. I tend to
think she's gold in color because her specialty is prolonging life and increasing resources, wisdom, and positive potential. The color gold is usually associated with the activity of increase, just as white is associated with pacifying.

This verse praises her color, her hand gestures, and her causes. As mentioned, her golden color illustrates increasing everything positive and useful
in life and in Dharma practice. In her left hand, she holds an open lotus that
symbolizes her enlightened state and her perfection of the ten far-reaching
attitudes. Sometimes six far-reaching attitudes are mentioned and sometimes
they're elaborated as ten. Six of them are listed here: giving (generosity), effort,
ethics, patience, concentration, and wisdom. The other four are aspiration
(prayer or vow), power, method, and exalted wisdom. The ten bodhisattva
stages or grounds span the path of seeing and the path of meditation, and on

each bodhisattva stage, a bodhisattva brings to perfection one of these ten far-reaching attitudes. Praising her causes means praising the six far-reaching attitudes and her completion of the accumulations of method and wisdom.

Sometimes the lotus stem she holds has a bud, a blossoming lotus, and a completely open lotus. These symbolize the Buddhas of the past, present and future. The bud is the Buddhas of the future, the blossoming flower is the Buddhas of the present, and the completely open lotus is the Buddhas of the past.

In general, the lotus symbolizes the blissful wisdom beyond the sorrow of cyclic existence. Her holding a lotus indicates that she possesses all virtuous qualities and abides in nirvana. When deities are seated on a lotus, the lotus generally symbolizes renunciation, the determination to be free from cyclic existence. The fact that deities sit or stand on a lotus means that they have mastered renunciation, which is the basis of the practice and the foundation of all other attainments.

> 4. Homage to you who crowns all Buddhas,
>   Whose action subdues without limit;
>   Attained to every perfection,
>   On you the bodhisattvas rely.

This is Tara, the Victorious Ushnisha of Tathagatas. The *ushnisha* is the crown protuberance on the Buddha's head. Its cause is a bodhisattva's great accumulation of positive potential on the path to Buddhahood. This Tara crowns all Buddhas, like the Buddhas' crown protuberance. She's gold in color, and her specialty is to neutralize poison, increase life, and counteract premature death. She can stop car accidents and untimely death—anything that might cause us to die before our full life span, as conditioned by our previous karma, has been lived out.

We praise Tara here because the Buddhas and bodhisattvas rely on her with great respect since she is the mother of all Buddhas. Being the mother of all Buddhas means that Tara is the embodiment of wisdom; it is wisdom that gives birth to all the Buddhas. "Attained to every perfection" indicates that she has mastered all ten perfections (far-reaching attitudes).

By respectfully carrying Tara on their crowns, Buddhas and bodhisattvas show us that we, too, should respect those who have good qualities. We may think that highly realized beings don't have to show respect to anyone because they have already developed great qualities, and therefore, others respect them. This is ego's way of thinking. In fact, the more someone's virtuous qualities increase, the more humble she becomes. Buddhas and bodhisattvas have great respect and appreciation for their teachers. If we find our arrogance increasing the more we "practice," then something is wrong. We're not actually practicing Buddhadharma; we're practicing Egodharma! The bodhisattvas of the ten stages, who are highly realized beings and have incredible powers, still rely on Tara. They're a good role model for us. If they rely on Tara, then certainly we need to. If they are humble, then of course we need to be.

This Tara symbolizes the forces that can subdue negative events in this life, thus bringing us happiness while we're still in cyclic existence. She also symbolizes the wisdom that eliminates the two obscurations—afflictive obscurations and cognitive obscurations—that prevent attaining our ultimate aims.

> 5. Homage to you whose TUTTARA and HUM
> Fill the realms of desire, form, and space.
> You crush seven worlds beneath your feet
> And have power to call all forces.

The name of this Tara is Tara Proclaiming the Sound of HUM, or Tara Summoning the Three Worlds. She's also gold, and her specialty is influencing and subjugating. This verse praises her ability to suppress adverse factors. She is slightly wrathful. At her heart is the syllable HUM, and around it is a mantra. The TUTTARA and HUM symbolize the wisdom realizing emptiness that is conjoined with great compassion.

With her feet, which also have this nature of wisdom and compassion, she presses on the seven realms. The seven realms are the hell beings, hungry ghosts, animals, humans, desire gods, form gods, and formless gods. Those seven comprise all the realms in cyclic existence. She's pressing them beneath her feet, which means that she's subjugating their cause and showing these beings the path to liberation. By teaching them about emptiness, she gives them the tools to free themselves from those rebirths. In that way, she shows them the path to liberation.

By the light radiating from the HUM and the mantra letters, by the sound of the mantra, and by stamping her feet, she shows the power to overcome these seven realms of cyclic existence. How does one overcome the seven realms? By developing the three principal aspects of the path, which are what Tara embodies. Thinking of Tara in this symbolic way, as the embodiment of qualities that we are trying to develop, prevents us from seeing her as an external God.

Tara draws sentient beings to her, brings them under her influence, and persuades them to practice the Dharma. With the activity of control or influence, Buddhas and bodhisattvas influence others and show them how to practice. Realized beings perform the activity of controlling sentient beings so that we'll actually listen to what they teach. Lots of times they try to influence us, and we block them out. We don't go to teachings, fall asleep during Dharma talks, and later don't make an effort to remember what was said. But enlightened ones with great compassion don't give up on us; they keep trying to get through to us.

They're trying to influence us, to hook us so they can teach us. But from our side, we need to do something. We need to make ourselves receptive vessels by purifying our negativities and accumulating positive potential. This is the purpose of reciting the seven-limb prayer, prostrating to the Thirty-five Confession Buddhas, and reciting the "Homage to the Twenty-one Taras." When we let ourselves be influenced by the Buddhas and bodhisattvas, our minds soften. We develop confidence, trust, and faith in the Three Jewels, which make our mind more receptive to what they teach. When we are receptive, we follow the instructions they give us, and by practicing, we attain the results—upper rebirth, liberation, and enlightenment.

Many of us have received lots of instructions on how to practice the Dharma and how to ease the pain of the afflictions. The reason we still have problems is not because we lack teachings but because we haven't put them into practice. When we get angry, do we apply the antidotes to anger? No, we call up our friend, bad-mouth the other person, and win our friend to our side. We know the antidotes to the negative emotions, but in the moment we forget them. This verse shows us that Tara is trying to influence us so that something will get through to us and we'll practice the instructions that we've received.

Sometimes our mind is completely overwhelmed by craving. We are obsessed, worrying about this, agonizing about that, wanting to be with somebody, fretting over the relationship. Is the relationship going to work, is it not going to work? How am I going to get this? What's going to happen? Our mind spins round and round our self-centered concerns. We've heard many teachings about how to subdue attachment—for example, recalling the disadvantages of cyclic existence and seeing that there's absolutely no happiness in cyclic existence. But when our mind is overpowered by craving and worry, do we contemplate the disadvantages of cyclic existence? No! Again, we call up our friend and cry, "Oh, I want this. This person is not being nice to me. I want to be with them so badly. They don't like me. What can I do? Poor me!" We neglect to see that our own attachment is the cause of our suffering.

When we're sick or harmed, meditating on this Tara is helpful. Think of light radiating from her body and from the HUM and the mantra; think of the sound of the mantra resonating from the mantra syllables. Imagine that these eliminate whatever sickness or harm you are experiencing.

6. Homage to you adored by Indra,
   Agni, Brahma, Vayu, and Ishvara,
   Praised in song by hosts of spirits,
   Zombies, scent-eaters, and yakshas.

This Tara is called Tara Victorious over the Three Worlds. She is ruby red, although in some cases she is reddish-black. Her specialty is to purify obscurations and negativities. In this verse, we praise her because the worldly gods offer their service to her. Written in the context of ancient Indian society where many people believed in the Hindu gods, this verse shows that these important gods pay respect to Tara. Indra is the king of gods; Agni is the god of fire; Brahma is the creator of the world; and Vayu is the creator of wind.

In addition, spirits led by Ganesh, zombies, who regard Ishvara as their lord, gandharvas, spirits who eat smells, and yakshas, whose leader is Vaishravana, honor Tara.

Westerners may wonder, "Who are these gods?" If we were to adapt this to our cultural context, the verse might be, "Homage to you adored by Jesus, Mary, Moses, Abraham, Mohammed, Zeus, Socrates, Plato, Rambo, Madonna, Freud, Dr. Laura, Clinton, Bush, and everyone in Star Wars." We can imagine that the Greco-Roman gods and all the non-human beings spoken of in Western culture—witches, gnomes, angels, and devils—all praise, respect, and pay homage to Tara.

The gods mentioned in the verse are powerful and have a glorious appearance. They've reached the pinnacle of worldly success, yet when they come close to Tara, they recognize their limits and lose their conceit. Becoming humble, they realize that they have to rely on her. This reminds us that even if we attain worldly success, power, fame, and prestige, as long as we're in cyclic existence we need to rely on the Buddha, Dharma, and Sangha to attain the happiness of liberation. Ultimately, everyone has to practice a path of wisdom and compassion. That worldly gods offer service to Tara illustrates that their doctrines are insufficient to attain liberation and that Tara has the correct view that leads to nirvana.

Tara tames the minds of some of the demons, zombies, and yakshas by drawing them close to her. But for those whose afflictions can't be subdued in that way, she has to be more forceful, employing fierce means to get them on the path. Destroying them means transferring their minds to a pure land or destroying the wrong views that they symbolize. Doing this is the function of the fierce-looking deities.

Although the worldly gods have many followers and teach various spiritual practices, they cannot lead us to nirvana, the state of lasting peace. To attain nirvana, we have to go beyond their doctrines and actualize the yogas in Tara's meditation practice. A similar point is seen in the Buddha's life story. After he renounced and left the home life, he learned from many teachers. Although he actualized all the samadhis they taught, he realized that his mind still wasn't liberated because it didn't have the correct view of emptiness. So he left those teachers and tried ascetic practices. They didn't bring nirvana either. Finally, he went to meditate under the bodhi tree where he gained the correct view of emptiness, which finally brought liberation.

Buddhism exists in cultures where other religions also exist, and referring to their gods and using some of those symbols is a skillful way of bridging the gap between an already-existing culture and Buddhadharma. Ancient Buddhist teachers made a place in Buddhism for deities from other religions and for other beings in whom common people believed. They aren't disparaged, but it's clear that their place is not the same as that of a Buddha. This illustrates that although these gods have some worldly power, they don't have the ultimate wisdom that liberates us from cyclic existence.

The process of cultural adaptation that naturally occurred as Buddhism spread throughout Asia may happen here, too. As Buddhism spreads in the West, what place will Moses, Abraham, Jesus, Virgin Mary, and Mohammed have? How will they be incorporated? One of the ways it seems that people are incorporating them is by considering them as bodhisattvas who skillfully manifest in that way to help people.

> 7. Homage to you whose TREY and PEY
>   Destroy external wheels of magic.
>   Right leg drawn in and left extended,
>   You blaze within a raging fire.

This is Tara Crushing Adversities or Crushing Disputants. Standing amidst a raging fire, she is black and fierce. Her specialty is *powa*—transference of consciousness to Akanishta pure land at the time of death.

She is praised for her ability to destroy opponents. She crushes the external threats of spirits, spells, and all external negative forces. She also destroys internal negative forces—disturbing attitudes and negative emotions—that impede our practice. We wouldn't have external hindrances if we didn't have internal ones. External ones only come about because we have created the karma to have them. Where did this karma come from? From the afflictions, which are internal hindrances. When our afflictions have been demolished, even if other beings try to harm us, we won't experience it as harm.

Tara pacifies others' negative thoughts by uttering the syllables TREY and

PEY. Uttering those syllables with a mind of wisdom and compassion also neutralizes magical substances and mantras used to cause harm. If this seems foreign to our cultural way of thinking, remember that in Tibet and ancient India as well as in many cultures nowadays, people believe in spells, spirits, and black magic. At one point someone tried to kill the thirteenth Dalai Lama with black magic, but the plot was discovered in time.

This Tara is standing up. Her bent right leg symbolizes compassion; her outstretched left leg symbolizes wisdom. In this way her body posture illustrates the essentials of the path to enlightenment. She presses down on the three realms and destroys those who give harm.

Essentially peaceful, this Tara may also be fierce. The raging fire surrounding her is the fire of wisdom that burns our ignorance, attachment, anger, jealousy, and pride. Especially when our mind is tumultuous and filled with all sorts of garbage, visualizing wisdom fire can have a good effect on the mind. Sometimes our mind is resistant when we try to apply Lamrim meditations to counteract our afflictions. When that happens, visualizing wisdom fire that burns our resistance is helpful.

This Tara is black and wrathful. In relation to the four activities, black is the color associated with subjugating or fierce activity. If others have evil thoughts toward us or try to harm is, then visualize Tara in front and imagine her roaring TREY and PEY, destroying their harm. She really hollers the mantras; she doesn't just sweetly smile and gently say, "TREY, PEY." She presses down on the harm-givers with her feet. Her wisdom flames completely burn them up and transfers their consciousness to the pure land.

Buddhas can manifest as fierce deities; their action of destroying is not motivated by anger but by compassion. In other words, they have tried peaceful, increasing, and influencing methods to remedy the situation, but these haven't worked. Somebody is creating tremendous havoc and causing sentient beings much pain, so Tara has to get tough because there's no other way. She acts fiercely out of compassion and transfers their consciousness to the pure land so that they will be free of the suffering their afflictions cause them. Certain yogis can perform such fierce methods, but there are stringent warnings about anyone unqualified trying them. If one lacks genuine compassion and pure realizations, then one can create the negative action of killing and be born in the hell realm. Having the ability to destroy is not a big deal—Osama bin Laden and George W. Bush have that—but being able to transfer the harmers' minds to a pure land requires great compassion and high yogic abilities.

Fierce deities symbolically show that there are a variety of ways to work with our afflictions. Sometimes we do so in a gentle fashion. But at other times, when our mind is being really ridiculous, we just have to say to ourselves, "Cut it out!" This resembles a deity's fierce actions.

It's similar to disciplining a child who is behaving like a brat. When a child is completely out of control, at some point we put our foot down. We stamp our foot down and say, "Enough is enough. This behavior is not appropriate and cannot continue." The child gets the message. Similarly, there are times in which we work with our afflictions in this way. We look at our own mind, not as "me," but as a wild, undisciplined child who is behaving like a brat. When we're sick of letting our mind go on a rampage, Tara comes, puts her foot down, and shouts, "This is enough!" It's very effective because it jolts us and makes us stop and examine what is happening in our minds.

Another unusual way to deal with our negative emotions is shown in the Chöd practice. There a practitioner imagines her afflictions appearing as demons. She invokes them in front of her, transforms her body into what they desire and with compassion, offers it to the demons. They are satisfied by this, relax, and stop harming others.

These practices give us a variety of methods to deal with our afflictions. As time goes on, we will develop the skill to know which technique is most suitable in a specific situation.

   8. Homage to you whose TURE destroys
      The great fears, the mighty demons.
      With a wrathful frown on your lotus face,
      You slay all foes without exception.

Starting with this eighth Tara, we praise the fierce sambhogakaya aspects. This Tara's name is Tara Who Crushes All Maras and Bestows Supreme Powers. She is golden in color and sits on a crocodile. She is fierce, and her specialty is the completion stage practice.

Here, we pay homage to her ability to destroy the four maras, or negative forces. The first mara is death, which severs this precious human life. The second is the five contaminated aggregates, which form our samsara. The third is our afflictions—disturbing attitudes and negative emotions—and the fourth is an external being called the son of the gods. He is like Cupid, who creates chaos and makes people confused. He also symbolizes the force of lust or arrogance. If we think of external beings who impede Dharma practice, Mao Tse-tung or Pol Pot would be modern examples. For us, they symbolize beings who wreak havoc for those who are trying to practice the Dharma.

Subduing the four maras means removing all the obscurations to enlightenment. The foes that Tara's wisdom slays are the two obscurations: the afflictive obscurations that prevent liberation and the cognitive obscurations that prevent omniscience. By saying TURE and showing her wrathful wrinkles, Tara destroys all outer, inner, and secret hindrances. The wrathful wrinkles make her face look like a lotus with petals; for that reason it's said, "her lotus face."

9. Homage to you beautifully adorned
   By the Three Jewels' gesture at your heart.
   Your wheel shines in all directions
   With a whirling mass of light.

The ninth Tara's name is Tara Granter of Boons, or Tara Wheel Governing and Granting All Desires. She's ruby red. This verse praises her hand gestures; her left hand is in the mudra or gesture of the Three Jewels. The thumb and ring finger touching symbolizes uniting method and wisdom on the path, and the three upward fingers represent Buddha, Dharma, and Sangha, the three refuges. Her specialty is consecration.

Her right hand is in the gesture of supreme giving, extended outward to help others and grant realizations. Her palms are adorned with wheels and the brilliant light radiating from the wheels overcomes all those who cause harm and act negatively. This light zaps them and stops them in their tracks.

The brilliance of her light also outshines that of other gods, vanquishing their arrogance. These beings might feel self-important, but Tara's wisdom light completely outshines theirs and subdues their arrogance. As recorded in many Mahayana sutras, before the Buddha speaks, light radiates from his body or from the curl at his forehead and spreads throughout many world systems. By radiating this light, all arrogant beings are subdued and come to listen to the Buddha speak. They realize that there is no way their light can compare with that of the Buddha's wisdom.

This reminds us that until enlightenment, we always have something to learn, so let's avoid becoming proud about our present abilities and knowledge. If we approach the Dharma with arrogance, learning becomes very difficult for us. Initially, some people who come to the Dharma are haughty, thinking, "I'm not suffering. I'm okay. My life is successful." But of course, it's not like that; otherwise, they wouldn't be coming to the Dharma center. This tough demeanor is a kind of defense against the truth, and it can be a barrier on the path.

The sutras contain stories of non-Buddhists who met the Buddha—for example, the story of the 500 matted-hair ascetics. Some of them were arrogant and wanted to compete with the Buddha. For example, some non-Buddhists who had clairvoyant and magical powers thought they were supreme and challenged the Buddha to a contest of miracle powers. Initially, the Buddha didn't accept, but they persisted in asking, so finally he consented. He knew this was the only way to subdue their arrogance. Of course, the Buddha's miraculous powers and clairvoyance completely overwhelmed theirs. They realized that their path was incomplete and gained great confidence in the Buddha. They cut their matted dreadlocks and became the Buddha's followers. This is the story behind one of the four great Buddhist holidays, the Day of Miracles, which falls on the full moon of the first lunar month.

Similarly today, people from other religions or those who follow no religion come to teachings given by His Holiness the Dalai Lama. These people aren't arrogant but are genuinely interested. During the talks they realize, "There's something special here." They don't necessarily become Buddhists, but they may apply some Buddhist teachings to the practice of their own tradition because they recognize the value in what His Holiness teaches.

A more insidious kind of arrogance may appear after we have heard some teachings. We know the words; we can recite the various categories and lists from different Dharma teachings; we know the names of the scriptures. We can say, "There are Four Noble Truths, and they relate to the two truths in this way…" We know the intellectual, academic answers to a few questions and become arrogant about our knowledge. We think we're doing really well—we're becoming great practitioners—but in actual fact, we're stuck because we lack humility and genuine faith in the Three Jewels. We think we have faith, but in actual fact the heart is tough with pride. We're using the Dharma to reinforce our sense of "I" with thoughts such as, "*I'm* such a good practitioner because *I* know this and that. *I* have studied this difficult philosophical text. *I* can teach the Middle Way view." We're not even aware that we're drowning in arrogance.

That becomes a big problem. That's why teachers sometimes have to speak strongly to some of their students, to shake them out of the arrogance that breeds complacency. Otherwise, the students go along thinking, "I know this. I know that. I've been practicing so long. I'm much more advanced than these other people. I can answer all the questions that they can't," and yet they aren't really practicing. It's very easy for this to happen, believe me.

Some people get to a point where they think, "I've studied this and that. I don't need to rely on teachers so much. I know as much as my teachers now. I explain the Dharma as well as they do to new people. I don't need to listen to their advice." This attitude is a huge interference in practice. Not only that, it is extremely dangerous for that person as well as for others. A self-inflated "teacher" can easily mislead students, thereby creating very negative karma and damaging the students' connection to the Dharma. Tara radiates her light to dispel this arrogance.

10. Homage to you, radiant and joyful,
    Whose crown emits a garland of light.
    You, by the laughter of TUTTARA,
    Conquer demons and lords of the world.

This Tara's name is Tara Dispelling All Sorrow, or Tara the Conqueror of the

Three Worlds. She is red, and her specialty is destroying maras, controlling the world of sentient beings, and fulfilling all wholesome wishes. This doesn't mean that if someone who greedily wants a BMW to show off to others prays to Tara, his prayer will come true. Rather, Tara will help fulfill our virtuous wishes, especially by instructing us on how to create the causes for happiness. Her ritual is for entering the mandala.

This verse praises her diadem, or crown, and her laughter. Understanding the aspirations and dispositions of various disciples, she radiates light from her crown that outshines other teachers with incorrect views. Laughing, she utters TUTTARA—"to liberate"—and brings the maras and the eight great gods of the world under her control by diminishing their pride. For me, the image of conquering by laughter is beautiful. She doesn't need bombs and guns to subdue harmful ones; her joyous laughter is sufficient. It makes self-important people begin to wonder, "I'm not joyous and laughing like Tara. Maybe there's something I can learn from her." Then she teaches them the Dharma, giving instructions that correspond to each individual's dispositions, interests, and level of the path. This ability to lead others on the path according to their individual inclinations is an ability unique to a fully enlightened one.

11.   Homage to you with power to invoke
      The assembly of local protectors.
      With your fierce frown and vibrating HUM,
      You bring freedom from all poverty.

This Tara is called Tara Summoner of All Beings, Tara Dispeller of All Misfortune, or Tara the Treasure of Wealth. She is the color of darkness. Her specialty is to increase enjoyments and wealth and eliminate poverty. Some people do Tara puja—meditation, offerings, and requests to Tara—for worldly wealth. This can bring about success in business and improve health. The real wealth, of course, is Dharma wealth, realizations of the path. If we pray for material wealth, it should be with the motivation to use it to benefit others, to maintain our life so we can practice the Dharma, to make offerings to those in need or to the Three Jewels, or to support practitioners. Tibetan monasteries do Tara pujas when they embark on new projects, such as building a new temple or opening a school. Lay people request Tara puja when they have obstacles to health or wealth. Often the obstacles cease after the puja.

Here Tara is praised because she can activate the ten directional protectors, the "local protectors." These protectors are inclined toward virtue and are leaders of other spirits. To activate them to do their various activities, she radiates light with hooks on the end of each beam. The hooks bring back the protectors, and she orders them to do beneficial work in the world. They naturally respond to her and listen to her instructions.

The wrathful wrinkles on her face flicker, and the light shining from the HUM at her heart brings liberation from all sorrow, poverty, and pain. We may think that's strange, "How can wrinkles and lights solve these problems?" Think about it: If you're depressed or feeling hopeless and then think of Tara, doesn't your mood change? Doesn't imagining her and thinking of her qualities pull you out of your stuck areas?

Poverty means not only lack of material wealth but also poverty of the Dharma. For example, we find ourselves living in a place where there are no teachers or teachings. To remedy this, we imagine Tara, generate positive aspirations, and pray to meet qualified teachers and perfect teachings.

Sometimes we have a sense of emotional poverty. We feel hollow inside and think nobody loves us. Often people cope with those unpleasant feelings through habitual, dysfunctional strategies. They distract themselves with shopping, eating, watching TV, and gambling. They medicate their suffering by drinking alcohol and taking drugs. Emotional poverty is an obstacle on the path. It draws our energy inward in self-pity and depression, which create obstacles in our mind.

Meditating on Tara can help heal these obstacles. Visualize Tara in front of you. Light radiating from her pours into you, filling up the emotional emptiness, the empty hole inside. Her light of wisdom and compassion heals your emotional poverty and you feel connected to Tara. Then Tara absorbs into you. She re-appears at your heart and you feel contented, confident, and connected to others. Loving, compassionate light from the small Tara at your heart radiates to other sentient beings. It touches them and brings them mental and physical ease.

This visualization changes the mind from feelings of self-pity, unworthiness, and lacking love to feelings of love, connectedness, and having something wonderful to share with others. As soon as we generate love toward others, the feeling of emotional poverty goes away. It's similar to St. Francis's prayer: May we think not how to be loved but how to give love.

12. Homage to you with crescent moon crown,
      All your adornments dazzling bright.
      From your hair-knot Amitabha
      Shines eternal with great beams of light.

This is Tara Giver of All Prosperity, also called Tara of Auspicious Light. She is gold, and we praise her crown ornaments. From her crescent moon crown ornament, white light radiates and eliminates sickness, suffering, sorrow, poverty, and depression. Then yellow light radiates from her crown ornament and performs the action of increasing. It enhances sentient beings' life span, positive potential, wisdom, and good qualities. In general, the color white is involved with the action of pacifying or subduing, and the color yellow is related to the action of increasing. Red is associated with control or influence, and black with fierce actions. Her ritual is the fire offering.

Amitabha Buddha rests on Tara's crown. Buddhist deities may be divided into five "families," related to the five Dhyani Buddhas. Amitabha Buddha is the head of the family to which both Tara and Chenresig belong. For this reason Amitabha sits on her crown. Amitabha is Tara's guru, her spiritual mentor. This reminds us to keep our spiritual teacher on our crown. In this way, we continuously respect our teacher and think of him or her being near us and guiding us when we need help.

From the small Amitabha on Tara's crown, light streams to all sentient beings, purifying their negative karma and inspiring them to gain Dharma realizations. Thinking like this is an expression of our compassion for others. We may wonder if imagining this does any good. Does it really help? It's hard to specify how much direct help others receive from our visualizations. Scientific studies have shown that people recover from illness and surgery more quickly when others pray for them. The mind is very powerful. When our mind is quiet, we can see from our own experience how powerful just one positive or negative thought can be. Visualizing and thinking in a loving way definitely has a powerful effect on us. When we train our mind in virtuous thoughts, we are happier and more readily act in kind ways to others. Since we exist interdependently with others, a change in our thoughts could have great effects on others as well as ourselves.

Some people may think a group of people generating positive aspirations together doesn't have any effect. They say that it is wishful thinking, that praying—that is, generating positive aspirations and wishes—brings no results. Would these same people say that a group of people thinking violent thoughts or racist thoughts has no effect?

When he was a bodhisattva, Amitabha made special vows to help lead ordinary sentient beings to the pure land. Through the power of his virtue, he established a pure land, Sukhavati, the Land of Great Bliss (Tib: *Dewachen*), where ordinary beings can be reborn. Once born there, it is easy to gain realizations because everything around us is conducive for practice.

13. Homage to you who dwells in a blazing wreath
     Like the fire at the end of this age.
     Your right leg outstretched and left drawn in,
     Joy surrounds you who defeats hosts of foes.

This is Tara the Ripener, or Tara Bestower of Maturity. She's ruby red, standing, and her specialty is to subdue hindrances and to protect from fear and danger. The verse praises her fierce posture of standing in a blazing wreath. "The fire at the end of this age" refers to the ancient Indian belief that this particular universe will cease in a conflagration. Some universes are destroyed by wind, others by water, and others by fire. Fire will destroy the desire realm of this universe, but not the form and formless realms. Because sentient beings have created the karma, new universes in cyclic existence will later arise. Tara's wisdom fire is unique: It destroys all the realms of cyclic existence. That is, the wisdom realizing emptiness burns the causes of cyclic existence—afflictions and karma—in such a way that they can never arise again. In that way, it liberates us.

Tara defeats all hosts of foes. The real foes are the afflictions that keep us bound in cycles of suffering. Arhats are called "foe destroyers" because they have destroyed the foes of afflictions that cause cyclic existence. Thus, joy surrounds Tara because not only has she destroyed these foes, but she has also vanquished the obscurations preventing full omniscience.

14. Homage to you whose foot stamps the earth
     And whose palm strikes the ground by your side.
     With a wrathful glance and the letter HUM
     You subdue all in the seven stages.

This Tara is called Tara the Wrathful Summoner, or Shaking, Frowning Tara. She is stamping her foot, saying, "Enough with the obstacles to liberation and enlightenment! Enough with suffering! I'm going to destroy these!" Her body is made of black light, and she stands amidst a protective circle. Forming a protective circle of light, she destroys interferences to the flourishing of the Dharma and interferences to the happiness and well-being of sentient beings. These two, the flourishing of the Dharma and the welfare of sentient beings, are linked because it's through the Dharma existing and flourishing in our world that sentient beings learn how to create constructive karma and thus experience happiness. What interferes with the flourishing of the Dharma? People who distort the Dharma teachings or who make up their own beliefs, call it Buddhism, and lead people on the wrong path. People who, through their political power, make laws that limit religious freedom, harass the monastic community, destroy monasteries, or burn scriptures also hinder the existence of the Buddha's teachings. In our world, unfortunately many of these activities are happening.

I heard of someone who made a beautiful tune for the Tara mantra but added an extra "Tara" to the mantra because it made the melody nice. This is not wise to do. Similarly, some people skip a topic they don't like very much when they teach or they re-interpret it so it agrees with their ideas and then teach it to others. This is very damaging for both the speaker and the listener. This Tara helps to prevent such activity. She also confronts and turns back physical obstacles such as disease and untimely death.

She is black and stands in a protective circle. This verse praises the light radiating from her syllable HUM. Her right foot ferociously stamps the earth, and her right hand is in the threatening mudra. She has a wrathful look. Selfishness and ignorance don't want to mess with her because she means business.

Radiating light from the syllable HUM at her heart destroys obstacles. On the palms of her hands and the soles of her feet is a HUM. Torrents of vajras, like a hailstorm, radiate from each HUM. It's like a shower of glowing, radiating wisdom vajras. The rain of vajras destroys all interferences and hindrances. They go to the bottom of the seven levels under the world, where Yama, the lord of death, is said to live. Destroying the lord of death symbolizes overcoming cyclic existence, the nature of which is impermanence and death.

The wrathful vajras radiating from her palms and soles, the threatening gesture of her right hand, and her stamping foot puts a halt to all the problems instigated by nagas, asuras, various spirits, and yamas. To make the meaning relevant to our culture, we could imagine her destroying street gangs, the Mafia, those dealing in arms, drugs, and nuclear material, al-Qaeda, those who misuse aid shipments, and anyone who damages sentient beings. When such difficulties exist in the world or in our life, doing this meditation and imagining the problems being subdued is very effective.

Verses 2 through 14 praise Tara's sambhogakaya (enjoyment body). The sambhogakaya is the aspect in which the Buddha appears to teach high-level bodhisattvas, those who have realized emptiness and appear in the form of deities. Next, we praise her dharmakaya (truth body), her omniscient mind.

15. Homage to the blissful, virtuous, peaceful one,
    Object of practice, nirvana's peace.
    Perfectly endowed with SOHA and OM,
    Overcoming all the great evils.

She is called Tara the Great Peaceful One and is white in color. There's an external washing or purifying ritual that goes with her practice, and her specialty is to pacify negative karma. The verse praises her speech and her dharmakaya mind. All her actions are done within the peace of nirvana.

The first two lines, "Homage to the blissful, virtuous, peaceful one, object of practice, nirvana's peace," outline some of the Mahayana paths to enlightenment. A path is a consciousness, not an external roadway. In other words, our mind becomes a path when it has developed certain realizations. There are five Mahayana paths—the paths of accumulation, preparation, seeing, meditation, and no more learning—that a practitioner develops sequentially.

"Blissful" refers to the path of accumulation, the first path. We enter this path when we first generate unfabricated, spontaneous bodhichitta every time we see or think about a sentient being. The path of accumulation is blissful because we have the taste of emptiness that comes through the first two wisdoms, the wisdoms of hearing and thinking about emptiness. Although our wisdom is not fully developed, it starts to cut through the elaborations of inherent existence and brings bliss in the mind.

"Virtuous" refers to the path of preparation. The demarcation between the path of accumulation and the path of preparation is when one has developed the union of *shamatha* (meditative quiescence) and *vipashyana* (special insight) focused on emptiness. Although one has realized emptiness, at this level it's a conceptual realization, an inference. One's perception of emptiness is not yet direct and non-conceptual.

"Peaceful" indicates the path of seeing. That's the point when one has direct, non-conceptual realization of emptiness and becomes an arya—a noble or superior one. At this point one begins to free one's mindstream from the acquired or artificial afflictions—those learned from erroneous philosophies—and their seeds. These are eliminated entirely so that they never return. The innate afflictions and their seeds haven't yet been eliminated, but they manifest very weakly, if at all, because one has the direct perception of emptiness when in meditative equipoise, and after meditative equipoise, one sees all phenomena as like illusions and so doesn't grasp them as inherently existent.

Although not explicitly mentioned in the verse, the fourth of the five Mahayana paths, the path of meditation, eliminates the innate level of afflictive obscurations that prevent liberation. These are the disturbing attitudes and negative emotions that have been with us since beginningless time. On the latter part of the path of meditation, one removes the cognitive obscurations that prevent Buddhahood. So there's a lot to do on the path of meditation.

"Nirvana's peace" refers to the fifth path, the path of no more learning, which is our final object of practice. This path pacifies all obscurations, and one becomes a Buddha, a fully enlightened one who has removed all defilements and generated all good qualities to the fullest. One now has actualized the three Buddha-bodies: the dharmakaya (truth body), sambhogakaya (enjoyment body), and nirmanakaya (emanation body). One has attained all this for the purpose of liberating all sentient beings from suffering and its causes.

The Sanskrit word "Buddha" was translated into Tibetan as *sanggye*; *sang* means "to cleanse," and *gye* connotes "to expand or increase." By means of the wisdom realizing the ultimate nature, emptiness, a Buddha has cleansed all defilements so they can never return and has expanded his or her wisdom to encompass all phenomena. A Buddha has also increased all good qualities to their maximum. When we imagine light and nectar coming from Tara into us, we think that they are doing two things: first, purifying and cleansing our defilements, and second, enhancing our good qualities, wisdom, and virtues. Do you see how our visualization and meditation on Tara relates to the meaning of *sanggye*?

"Perfectly endowed with SOHA and OM, overcoming all the great evils" means we recite SOHA and OM, the first and last syllables of Tara's mantra, and everything in-between. So the phrase indicates reciting Tara's ten-syllable peaceful mantra, OM TARE TUTTARE TURE SOHA. By reciting, integrating, and actualizing the meaning of the mantra, the greatest evil, which is the ignorance grasping at true existence, is destroyed. This doesn't mean that reciting Tara's mantra without doing anything else leads to liberation. If that were so, a tape recorder could be enlightened before us because it can chant more mantras! Reciting her mantra means saying it with the understanding of the three principal aspects of the path. We have to make effort to actualize the meaning of the mantra, which is the entire path to enlightenment.

Another interpretation is that "blissful" refers to freedom from the truth of suffering, and "virtuous" refers to freedom from the ten destructive actions that cause these sufferings. "Peaceful" refers to completely pacifying all afflictions. "Nirvana's peace" refers to non-abiding nirvana—that is, the nirvana of a Buddha or full enlightenment. The nirvana of an arhat and the nirvana of a Buddha are different in that an arhat attains nirvana for his or her own benefit. From a Mahayana point of view, that's considered abiding in a peaceful state with self-complacency, that is, being content with liberating just oneself. A bodhisattva, on the other hand, wants to eliminate both the afflictive and cognitive obscurations and attain full enlightenment in order to be of the utmost benefit to all sentient beings. Thus, non-abiding nirvana means one doesn't abide in cyclic existence or in self-complacent peace, the liberation of an arhat, but attains full enlightenment.

If we think of the qualities of Tara's dharmakaya mind and recite her mantra, we'll free ourselves from true suffering and true causes. Simply meditating on the mantra's meaning alleviates suffering. For example, saying the mantra and thinking about its meaning frees us from a bad mood. Try it! The next time you're grouchy, grumpy, or feeling down, imagine Tara—serene, joyful, and radiating green light—and say her cheerful mantra. Imagine light flowing from her into you and all sentient beings. See what happens to your bad mood.

The following verses praise her activities.

16. Homage to you with joyous retinue,
     You subdue fully all enemies' forms.
     The ten-letter mantra adorns your heart,
     And your knowledge-HUM gives liberation.

This is Tara Destroyer of All Attachment. Coral red, she amplifies the power of mantras and cuts negative thoughts that impede the increase of positive energy. This verse praises the activity of both her peaceful and fierce mantras. When she teaches the Dharma through the action of her speech, all afflictions are pacified. This doesn't mean that Tara teaches and afflictions vanish on their own. It means that from their side, sentient beings respond to the teachings and put them into practice. We need to make effort to cease our afflictions and develop our good qualities.

"Knowledge-HUM" is the seed syllable of Tara's wrathful manifestation, while TAM is for her peaceful manifestations. HUM indicates her fierce mantra

OM NAMA TARE NAMO HARE HUM HARE SOHA. By the power of both her peaceful mantra, OM TARE TUTTARE TURE SOHA, and her wrathful mantra, OM NAMA TARE NAMO HARE HUM HARE SOHA, all self-grasping of persons and self-grasping of phenomenon cease.

To meditate on this fierce Tara, imagine her in front of you with the knowledge syllable HUM at her heart. Around it stand the syllables of the fierce (wrathful) mantra. Light radiates from the mantra, flowing into us, pervading the environment, and eliminating all internal and external adverse circumstances. This visualization can be combined with the practice of transforming all adverse circumstances into the path, as taught in the thought training (*lo-jong*) texts. This is very effective to transform our experiences.

17. Homage to TURE with stamping feet,
     Whose essence is the seed-letter HUM,
     You cause Meru, Mandara, and Vindhya,
     And all three worlds to tremble and shake.

This is Tara Accomplisher of All Bliss. She is orange, and her specialty is to bind thieves and to eliminate the power of black magic mantras. This verse praises her fierce activity of shaking the three worlds—below, on, and above the earth. From the primordial sound HUM appears TURE, which means Tara, and her pounding feet make everything in the external world tremble. This indicates her power, the power of the Buddha's enlightening activity. When the great mountains like Meru and so forth shake, the evil beings are scared. It's similar to experiencing an earthquake. Our feeling of permanence is shaken, and we begin to think about impermanence and become more humble. In a similar way, Tara's actions humble sentient beings.

By humbling evil beings and any evil thoughts in our own minds, Tara pacifies obstacles to the spread of the Dharma and the happiness of sentient beings. The chapter in *Transforming the Heart* (by Geshe Jampa Tegchok) on the Four Noble Truths talks about the sixteen erroneous conceptions associated with the Four Noble Truths. Think that Tara destroys those sixteen erroneous conceptions and brings about the sixteen accurate ones. The distorted conceptions concerning the truth of suffering are holding (1) impermanent things as permanent, (2) things that are suffering in nature as happiness, (3) impure things as pure, and (4) phenomena that are selfless as having a self. Tara's wisdom is the opposite of these four, so it pacifies these as well as the other twelve misconceptions.

Through the explanation on this Tara, the importance of understanding and practicing the Lamrim is evident. We must bring the Lamrim into our tantric practices and visualizations. This gives us more to contemplate while visualizing and while reciting mantra. It makes our practice real Dharma instead of just a pleasant visualization. We must remember that the Lamrim is the essence of Tara.

18. Homage to you who holds in your hand
     A moon like a celestial lake.
     Saying TARA twice and the letter PEY,
     You dispel all poisons without exception.

This Tara is Tara the Victorious. She is white, and her specialty is to dispel diseases caused by nagas, such as leprosy, tumors, and boils. She also pacifies diseases caused by poisons, such as toxins in the environment, air pollution, and food poisoning. This verse praises her activities that dispel the poisons of the world and the environment. As our planet becomes more polluted, new diseases associated with the environment are identified. The practice of this Tara is very good for those.

The "moon like a celestial lake" symbolizes her power to eliminate not only external poisons but also the three poisonous attitudes of ignorance, anger, and attachment, and their effects—all the suffering of cyclic existence. She holds the moon in her right hand. "Saying TARA twice and the letter PEY" refers to reciting a special modified mantra OM TARE TUTTARE TURE PEY. PEY indicates dispelling harm. It's sharp, forceful, and ejects harms.

19. Homage to you on whom the kings of gods,
     The gods themselves, and all spirits rely.
     Your armor radiates joy to all;
     You soothe conflicts and nightmares as well.

This Tara is Tara Consumer of All Suffering, or Tara the Invincible Queen. She is white, and her specialty is to free from poison. This verse praises her activity of dispelling conflict, bad thoughts, and nightmares.

In the Hindu worldview, Indra is the king of the desire realm gods, and Brahma is the king of the form realm gods. As mentioned before, they were given a role within the Buddhist worldview, but they don't have the qualities of a Buddha. Acknowledging Tara's superior qualities, these gods bow their heads in respect and pay homage to her. With the splendor of her inspiration, she dispels the nightmares and conflicts of those who devotedly and single-pointedly take to heart her armor—in other words her peaceful and fierce forms and her peaceful and fierce mantras. Cyclic existence is full of conflicts—in the Middle East, in our nation's capital, in our community, in our family, at our workplace, inside ourselves. Tara—that is, wisdom and compassion—dispels these conflicts.

If you wake up in the middle of the night from a terrifying dream, take refuge in Tara. Turn to loving kindness, compassion, and wisdom to guide you. When we view the appearances in a nightmare with wisdom, we realize that there's nothing there but an appearance. There's no grotesque monster chasing us.

If we have negative thoughts—uncontrolled, troublesome, violent, or lustful thoughts that we don't usually have—if we are depressed or suicidal or have a lot of bad omens and signs, relying on this particular Tara is effective. She helps to free us from all of that.

20. Homage to you whose eyes, the sun and moon,
     Radiate with pure brilliant light;
     Uttering HARA twice and TUTTARA
     Dispels extremely fearful plagues.

This Tara is Tara the Source of All Attainments. She is orange and grants the power to make oneself invisible. She also cures horrible diseases. This verse praises her activity of dispelling fever and epidemic diseases. Just as chronic fevers and certain illnesses drag on and one is not able to shake them off, so too, cyclic existence drags on and flares up. Here, her right eye is like the sun and symbolizes her fierce aspect. Her left eye is gentle like the moon, symbolizing her peaceful aspect. "Uttering HARA twice" means reciting the fierce mantra (OM NAMA TARE NAMO HARE HUM HARE SOHA) and "uttering...TUTTARA" means reciting the peaceful mantra (OM TARE TUTTARE TURE SOHA). By reciting these two, powerful illnesses are overcome.

When we are ill, thinking of both the fierce and the peaceful aspects of Tara and reciting both mantras are helpful. This meditation is good for illnesses such as cancer, AIDS, environmental pollution, new diseases that are appearing now, and illnesses that are very difficult to cure.

In Chinese and Tibetan medicine, illnesses are either heating or cooling. If it's a cooling illness and one has too much cooling energy, then meditate on the fierce Tara with her right eye like the sun and it heats you up. If you have too much heat energy, then meditate on the peaceful Tara with her left eye like the moon. This is cooling just like moonbeams are cooling. Imagine such light coming into you or whoever is sick, curing all illnesses.

> 21. Homage to you, adorned with three natures,
>   Perfectly endowed with peaceful strength.
>   You destroy demons, zombies, and yakshas;
>   O TURE, most exalted and sublime!

This Tara is Tara the Perfector. She is white, and her specialty is sky-going. In other words, she takes you to the Akanishta Pure Land in this very life. This verse praises her activity of subduing evil spirits and zombies. Her three natures are her body, speech, and mind appearing as OM, AH, HUM. OM is at her crown chakra, AH at her throat chakra, and HUM at her heart chakra. These pacify internal poisons such as the afflictions, and external poisons or interferences such as demons, zombies, yakshas, and spirits who take away the power of medicine, the power of our body, or the power of food. These beings can also cause mental illness. Because of some karma from a past life with a particular being who was reborn as a spirit, a person can experience mental disturbances or mental illness. This Tara can be very effective in dispelling that.

Although many of these verses show Tara ostensibly banishing external harms, my guess is that on a deeper level, these are analogies for internal and secret obscurations that are to be overcome by the five Mahayana paths. The explanation above of the five paths is according to the sutra viewpoint. Highest yoga tantra has its unique way of explaining them. We should not be satisfied by a superficial understanding of the words, but should try to gain a deeper understanding and then actualize those meanings.

> Thus, the root mantra is praised,
> And twenty-one homages offered.

We praise her mantra and offer the twenty-one homages to the twenty-one Taras.

THE CONDENSED PRAISE

If we cannot recite the long "Homage to the Twenty-one Taras," reciting the condensed praise[5] is fine. This praises the mantra—that is, it praises her realizations. The short verse is:

> OM to the transcendent subduer, Arya Tara, I prostrate.
> Homage to the glorious one who frees with TARE;
> With TUTTARA you calm all fears;
> You bestow all success with TURE;
> To the sound SOHA I pay great homage.

---

5. Translated from the Tibetan by Ven. Sangye Khadro and reprinted here with her permission.

Benefits of Reciting the "Homage"

FOLLOWING the twenty-one praises are some verses that speak about the benefits of reciting the "Homage."

Those endowed with perfect and pure respect for these deities, the intelligent who recite these praises with supreme faith, both in the evening and upon waking at dawn, will have the fearlessness bestowed upon them by this remembrance. After being purified of all evils completely, they will attain the destruction of all lower realms. And the seven million conquering Buddhas will quickly grant them every empowerment. Thus, they will attain greatness and go forth to the ultimate state of supreme Buddhahood. As a result, all violent poisons, whether abiding within or spreading to others, that they have eaten or drunk will by this remembrance be completely removed, and they will eliminate completely affliction by spirits, epidemics, poisons, and all various sufferings. If for oneself or for the sake of others these praises are said sincerely two, three, or seven times, those wishing a child will have one, and those wishing wealth will attain this as well. Without obstruction, all their wishes will be granted, and every single hindrance will be destroyed as it arises.[6]

6. Translator unknown

The outline of the benefits is in four sections:

1. Distinction of the thought
2. Distinction of the time
3. Actual explanation of the benefits
4. Condensed statement of the benefits in numerical terms

The distinction of thought is expressed by:

> Those endowed with perfect and pure respect for these deities, the
> intelligent who recite these praises with supreme faith, both in the
> evening and upon waking at dawn, will have the fearlessness be-
> stowed upon them by this remembrance. After being purified of all
> evils completely, they will attain the destruction of all lower realms.

Intelligent ones recite the "Homage" with sincere devotion. With wisdom
understanding the symbolic meaning and the Dharma meaning, they are able
to focus on both meanings one-pointedly. They are not filled with doubt or
distraction.

The section on distinction of time starts with "both in the evening and
upon waking at dawn." The intelligent ones remember Tara's three kayas
(Buddha-bodies)—dharmakaya, sambhogakaya, and nirmanakaya, recite her
praises and mantras, and focus on Tara's peaceful aspects in the morning and
her wrathful aspects in the evening. Doing this brings the benefit of becoming fearless, free from hindrances, sickness, demons, untimely death, and
other difficulties in this life. Because they concentrate with faith and respect
and do purification one-pointedly, reciting the "Homage" counteracts their
negative karma and ceases all bad migrations in future lives. Thus it says,
"After being purified of all evils completely, they will attain the destruction
of all lower realms." This line talks about the benefit for future lives.

The actual explanation starts with:

> And the seven million conquering Buddhas will quickly grant them
> every empowerment. Thus, they will attain greatness and go forth to

the ultimate state of supreme Buddhahood. As a result, all violent poisons, whether abiding within or spreading to others, that they have eaten or drunk will by this remembrance be completely removed, and they will eliminate completely affliction by spirits, epidemics, poisons, and all various sufferings.

"Quickly" in the first line means the benefit will accrue in this lifetime. The intelligent ones will be empowered by seven million Buddhas with light rays or streams of nectar. Let's generate strong aspirations in Tara's presence and make sincere prayers to Tara, not praying to her like someone would pray to God, but contemplating the correct understanding of who Tara is. She is empty of inherent existence, but she also appears, like an illusion. She is the union of emptiness and dependent arising, the union of the two truths—she doesn't exist ultimately, but she does exist conventionally. In this way, meditation on Tara becomes contemplation of the two truths.

Because intelligent ones meditate in this way, seven million Buddhas who stay with Tara come and grant empowerment. Practitioners will have an excellent place to live, a healthy and attractive body, and good possessions, which they use for the purpose of attaining enlightenment. They will gain the common attainments—eight *siddhi*s such as flying, reading others' minds, and making oneself invisible. They will be free of harms from human beings and harms from spirits and troublemakers. They will also attain the supreme attainment, Buddhahood. These are the two attainments: (1) Mundane attainments are various clairvoyant powers that are used for the benefit of others, and (2) the supreme attainment is full enlightenment—total freedom and full capability to work most effectively for others.

Think about the goals of the three levels of practitioners. The initial practitioner seeks a fortunate rebirth, the middle seeks liberation, and the advanced aims for Buddhahood. Paying homage to Tara in the proper way helps to purify the obstacles to attaining these three. The defilements are the poisons that prevent us from attaining these. In particular, erroneous views are poisonous, because they make us relinquish practicing the Dharma. Erroneous views include thinking, "Past and future lives absolutely do not exist. There's no such thing as karma. People are inherently selfish so there's no use practicing Dharma because we can't change. The world is completely screwed up, and there's nothing that I can do about it, so why try?" All these are distorted views about conventional or ultimate truths, and they cause us to abandon the Dharma. One who gives up practice creates more negative karma because he is no longer mindful about his actions. This results in more suffering. So let's examine our minds carefully and avoid any erroneous views.

Reciting the "Homage" calms those poisonous distorted views as well as poisons from food, drink, snakes, scorpions, and infectious diseases.

> If for oneself or for the sake of others these praises are said sincerely two, three, or seven times, those wishing a child will have one, and those wishing wealth will attain this as well. Without obstruction, all their wishes will be granted, and every single hindrance will be destroyed as it arises.

This is a condensed statement of the benefits in numerical terms. This practice may be done for ourselves or for others who we know are having difficulties. When it says "two, three, or seven times," two refers to the basis, in other words a practitioner having the two qualities of sharp faculties and appreciative faith. This means a practitioner who is intelligent, open-minded, has great faith based on investigation, and who is sincere in his or her motivation.

Three indicates the times when the "Homage" is recited: morning, noon, and night. Seven indicates the number of times that one recites it. Some texts say to recite the "Homage" seven times each of the three times: morning, noon, and evening. Another interpretation is to do it seven times in each of the three times for three weeks. However, whether we recite the "Homage" once or many times, the quality of our mental state while chanting is the most important element determining the value of our action. Chanting the "Homage" once with sincerity and concentration transforms our mind more and creates greater positive potential than chanting it twenty-one times with a distracted mind or with an attitude of obligation.

Reciting the "Homage" in this way makes one fearless, helps one attain all virtuous desires, and subdues all objects of abandonment. "Those wishing a child will have one" refers to two cases. One is ordinary people who would like to have a baby. The second is Dharma teachers who would like a qualified disciple to train and to whom they can pass the lineage.

"All their wishes will be granted..." It may seem contradictory to the Buddha's teaching on non-attachment and simplicity of lifestyle for someone to pray for wealth and for all his wishes to be fulfilled. There are two ways to see this. One is that Tara helps people at their own level. In other words, if someone seeks wealth or worldly success and that person has created the karma for that, Tara will help him. Someone who is more spiritually astute sees that craving for these things is the source of suffering. That person will pray to Tara, aspiring that her craving and attachment be subdued so that she can progress on the path. According to this person's wish, Tara will help as well.

However, if someone with a non-virtuous intention prays to Tara to receive wealth, power, or to have his wishes fulfilled, Tara will not facilitate that. Tara's compassion is to alleviate suffering, not to enable someone to create more!

The second way to see these verses is that "wealth" may refer to the four requisites of life—food, shelter, clothing, and medicine—to be able to pursue Dharma practice without worry. This person's prayer for wealth is for the sake of Dharma, for the sake of others. He may also pray for wealth to be able to set up a soup kitchen, homeless shelter, or monastery. "Wealth" may also mean spiritual wealth, that is, realizations of the path. This internal wealth is the true wealth that satisfies all desires and fulfills all wishes. Thus, "wishes" may refer to temporal wishes—those benefiting us in cyclic existence—and ultimate wishes—liberation and enlightenment.

"Every single hindrance will be destroyed as it arises" means that new hindrances won't arise, and those already arisen will be destroyed. Those destroyed will never arise again.

This concludes the explanation of the benefits of doing this practice with sincerity and concentration, constantly cultivating a proper understanding of its meaning. Thinking that one could have a child and attain wealth due to reciting this prayer may initially seem like magical thinking. But when we engage in Dharma practice, contemplate the qualities of a Buddha, and exert effort to cultivate those qualities, our mind becomes very virtuous. The power of that virtue purifies negative karma, which prevents our wishes from being fulfilled. Of course, it doesn't mean that we say this prayer once or twice and suddenly an illness is cured or one receives an unexpected inheritance. There have to be other causes and conditions to bring about the results to which we aspire.

When I've done Tara practice to clear obstacles for a beneficial purpose, it's had a good effect. Try it yourself, and see how doing this recitation and contemplation affects your experience.

"A Song of Longing for Tara, the Infallible"

BY LAMA LOBSANG TENPEY GYALTSEN

T HE FOLLOWING is a request prayer to Tara, "A Song of Longing for Tara, the Infallible" (Tib: *Dung bo lu may ma*) written by Lama Lobsang Tenpey Gyaltsen.[7] It was translated by Lama Thubten Yeshe in February 1979, when he gave the Chittamani Tara initiations and teachings to a group of us at Kopan Monastery. In Lama's style, this may not be a literal translation, and words may be added to clarify the meaning. These verses deeply touched me at the time and continue to do so.

Lama Lobsang Tenpey Gyaltsen was born in 1836 and was recognized as the incarnation of Gomgan of Hormo. I find it remarkable that he wrote these verses when he was eighteen or nineteen. His mind was in a completely different place than my mind was at that age! He clearly had meditation experience and a strong connection with Tara. In fact, he speaks of her here as his personal guru.

> From my heart I bow to Divine Mother Tara, essence of love and compassion, the most precious objects of refuge gathered into one. From now until I reach enlightenment, hook me with your great love and kindness to liberate me.

7. "A Song of Longing" was translated by Lama Thubten Yeshe. Reprinted with kind permission from Lama Yeshe Wisdom Archives

By the witness of the Three Jewels, not just from my mouth but from the depths of my innermost heart and bones, I pray to you morning and evening. Show your blissful face to me, Loving One. Grant me the nectar of your speech.

Great gurus and small gurus cheat us with their made-up teachings, selling Dharma, teaching without comprehension, not observing who is qualified and who is not, being concerned about their own happiness and the eight worldly concerns. Since I can no longer trust friends of this degenerate age, you are my principal guru. Inspire me, Divine Mother, essence of love. Arouse the great power of your compassion and think of me.

I take refuge in you, Tara; like you, no Buddha could ever deceive me. But understanding the odd character of these times, most Buddhas have gone into the bliss of nirvana. Even though they have great compassion, we have no connection. Since for me there are no other deities, you are my principal deity. Bestow realizations upon me, Divine Mother, essence of love. Arouse the great power of your compassion and think of me.

Most Dharma protectors do not show their powers. Tired of those who invoke them, they do not act. Other protectors, lacking insight but proud of their power, may be friendly for a while but will later do me harm. Since I cannot rely on other protectors, you are my principal protector. With divine action, Wisdom Mother, essence of love, arouse the great power of your compassion and think of me.

To ordinary view the names of objects are the same as their meaning. Like this, they produce afflictions and bind us to samsara. When it is time to die, unless I understand the true nature, could a wish-fulfilling gem enable me to carry even a sesame seed with me? Since I do not trust in illusions, you are my real richness. Please grant my desires, Divine Mother, essence of love. Arouse the great power of your compassion and think of me.

I cannot rely on non-virtuous friends for even a day. They pretend to be close to me and all the while have in mind the opposite. They are friends when they wish it and enemies when they don't. Since I cannot trust in this kind of friend, you are my best friend. Be close to me, Divine Mother, essence of love. Arouse the great power of your compassion and think of me.

You are my guru, my yidam, my protector, my refuge, my food, my clothes, my possessions, and my friend. Since your divine quality is everything to me, let me spontaneously achieve all that I wish.

Although I am overwhelmed by my habitual, uncontrolled mind, please cut these self-centered thoughts so I will be able to give my body and my life millions of times without difficulty to each sentient being. Inspire me to be able to develop this kind of compassion to benefit all.

Empower me to cut the root of samsara, self-grasping, and to understand the pure doctrine, the most difficult middle way, free from the errors of extremes.

Inspire me to practice as a bodhisattva, turning away from what is worldly, dedicating all my virtues to teaching living beings, never for even one instant thinking of just my own happiness. Let me wish to attain Buddhahood for the benefit of all.

Empower me to actualize as much as possible the most subtle vows and to keep them without a careless mind, thus becoming the most perfect bodhisattva.

Outwardly, let me be simple in my practice, while inwardly, actualize the depth of the diamond vehicle with the strong wish to practice the two stages. Inspire me to attain enlightenment quickly for the benefit of all.

Divine Wisdom Mother Tara, you know everything about my life— my ups and downs, my good and bad. Think lovingly of me, my only mother.

I give myself and all who trust in me to you, Divine Wisdom Mother Tara. Being completely open to you, let us be born in the highest pure land. Set me there quickly with no births in between.

May the hook of your compassion and your skillful means transform my mind into Dharma and transform the minds of all beings, whoever they are. They have all been my mother, the mother of one unable to follow the Conqueror's teachings.

By reciting this prayer three times a day and by remembering the Divine Wisdom Mother Tara, may I and all beings who are connected to me reach whatever pure land we wish.

May the Three Jewels and especially the Divine Wisdom Mother, whose essence is compassion, hold me dear until I reach enlightenment. May I quickly conquer the four negative forces.

If, as long as you live, you recite this prayer three times every day, not just from the mouth (in words only) but strongly linked with your mind, you will have close connection and will see Tara's face. No hindrances will be experienced and all wishes will be fulfilled. You will have a close relationship with all Buddhas and bodhisattvas, and they will hold you dear. If you recite the "Homage to the Twenty-one Taras" and this prayer, you will attain the Divine Liberating Mother.

Colophon: This prayer to Venerable Tara, in heart words making his own requests and also non-deceptive to others, was composed by the Buddhist monk Lobsang Tenpey Gyaltsen, in his nineteenth year, the Water Mouse year (1852), on the third day of the miracle month (second month of the lunar calendar) at Bengar Namgyal Ling. It is sure to have great benefit.

Reflections on "A Song of Longing for Tara, the Infallible"

VERSE 1: THE THREE JEWELS

From my heart I bow to Divine Mother Tara, essence of love and compassion, the most precious objects of refuge gathered into one. From now until I reach enlightenment, hook me with your great love and kindness to liberate me.

"FROM MY HEART" indicates that we feel deep respect and admiration when we bow to Tara. We're not doing some empty ritual. When we do certain prayers or practices repeatedly, doing them with feeling can be a challenge. We easily fall into saying them, "blah, blah, blah," and then complain, "My practice isn't going well. I'm spinning my wheels and nothing's happening."

This may be because we space out and aren't concentrating. Our mouth is doing one thing, but our mind is doing another. We are distracted and think of something else—for example, what we're going to do that day—while reading a prayer. To recite a prayer or look at a friend with our heart, we must remind ourselves to bring our attention back to what we're reading, to pay attention to the words we're saying, and to feel their meaning.

Similarly, when we know somebody well, we sometimes stop appreciating them. We see them at breakfast and say, "Hi, dear," and proceed to read the back of the Cheerios box while eating our cereal. When we finish eating, we say, "Bye, dear," and go out the door. We take our dear ones for granted when we're too familiar with them.

Approaching everything freshly, with appreciation and interest, is the meaning of beginner's mind. This fresh approach makes our encounters with people rewarding. Each time we see someone, we remember that this is a fresh encounter, something new. This person in front of us is a living being to cherish. In the same way, even though we recite the same prayers every day, each time we say them is a new experience. It's not the same as when we said it yesterday. We have a new opportunity to connect with the Three Jewels, so we need to pay attention to what we're reading and say it from our heart.

Tara is called the "mother of all Buddhas" because she is the embodiment of the wisdom realizing emptiness; this wisdom is what gives birth to all Buddhas. Calling her "Mother" also indicates feelings of closeness and trust. We feel comfortable with Tara; we can relax around her and don't put on a good image in her presence in order to make her think we're someone we aren't. Rather, we know that as a Buddha, she won't judge us, so we are totally honest with Tara. This lets us be nourished by her wisdom and compassion.

Symbolically, the right side of the body correlates with the method or compassion aspect of the path. Method may also be represented by the male. The left side correlates with the wisdom aspect of the path, which in other instances is also represented by the female. When we see the tantric deities in union, the male represents compassion and the female, wisdom. This is the opposite of our usual associations in the West, where we think of women as being compassionate and men being knowledgeable. Switching the associations in this way is good for us. It prevents us from getting stuck in preconceptions about gender. However, this tantric symbolism doesn't mean that ordinary women are wiser and ordinary men are more compassionate.

The "essence of love and compassion" is what Tara is all about. You may wonder, "I thought Tara, as a female, represents wisdom and male deities represent compassion and now you're saying that Tara's essence is compassion." Let's not make the symbolism concrete and fabricate more preconceptions. All Buddhas have both wisdom and compassion. Calling her the essence of love and compassion reminds us of the traits we admire in her so that we will direct our energy into developing these qualities in our own mind.

"The most precious objects of refuge gathered into one" highlights that Tara embodies all three objects of refuge—Buddha, Dharma, and Sangha. Here, her mind represents the Buddha, her speech the Dharma, and her body the Sangha. This is one way of seeing the Three Jewels as gathered into that one particular figure. In another way, Tara's mind is the Dharma refuge—true cessations and true paths. She has realized emptiness directly and, as an arya, is the Sangha. Because her mind is free from all defilements and endowed with all qualities, she is also the Buddha.

"From now until I reach enlightenment, hook me with your great love and kindness to liberate me." I like the image of a hook, because it aptly describes the situation. Our minds get hooked on objects of attachment, anger, and jealousy. Friends, enemies, our reputation—these are like rings, and our disturbing emotions hook them and bind us to them in a tense relationship.

Here our genuine spiritual aspiration becomes a ring and we request Tara, "Please hook that ring! Hook my deep spiritual longing and aspirations. I know my life has deep meaning, and I want to be close to your wisdom and compassion. Due to your bodhichitta, teach and guide me in order to liberate me from this quagmire of preconceptions that causes me suffering and makes me inflict misery on others. Teach me how to overcome disturbing attitudes and negative emotions that perpetuate cyclic existence." When we say this from the heart, we get in touch with that side of ourselves that genuinely seeks liberation and enlightenment.

When we are out of touch with our sincere aspiration for enlightenment, our practice becomes rote. Neglecting to nurture our spiritual side, we become preoccupied with what's going on around us, and our energy disperses into busyness. "I have an appointment at nine, and a meeting at ten. I've got to pick up the kids at eleven and meet my colleague for lunch at twelve. And, by the way, I want to become a Buddha. Oh my gosh, look what time it is. I'd better say this prayer quickly. 'I take refuge....' Okay, finished. Glad that's done. Some day I'll go on retreat and slow down and do my practice properly, but right now there are too many other things to take care of." Whew! We wonder why our practice seems a little dry, while meanwhile our mind races around. We have to slow down and come back to our own spiritual yearning.

The Four Seals

Remembering the four seals—the four characteristics that seal a teaching as a Buddhist practice—helps to center us and invoke our spiritual yearning. These four are:

> All compounded phenomenon are impermanent.
> All contaminated phenomena are suffering in nature.
> All phenomena are selfless.
> Nirvana is peace.

All compounded phenomena are impermanent. Everything that is produced or compounded comes about due to causes and conditions. Therefore, it is impermanent—that is, it changes moment by moment. Why? Since the causal energy is changing each moment, the result must also be in the nature of change. Since the causal energy comes to an end, so must its result.

At the beginning of the day, it's good to reflect, "Everything that arises due to causes and conditions is transient. I'm changing moment to moment. My friends are transient and changing moment to moment. All the things I'm trying to achieve are transient, impermanent, and changing. Everything I crave is transient, impermanent, and changing. Every person, object, and situation I don't like is transient, impermanent, and changing." Thinking in this way very quickly helps us to see there's no use clinging to any of these things. Letting our negative emotions hook into any of these things is useless since they're all changing into something else.

This doesn't mean that we stop caring about others or that we become apathetic. Rather, we see that getting worked up, aggravated, stressed, and anxious about these things is inappropriate. It's like trying to stop a waterfall from flowing or the wind from blowing. When things are in the nature of change, the only appropriate response is to relax and try to guide how they change with compassion.

All contaminated phenomena are in the nature of suffering (dukkha). Contaminated means under the influence of the ignorance that grasps at inherent existence, the misconception that is the root of cyclic existence and that fuels all other disturbing emotions. This ignorance actively misconceives how all persons and phenomena exist. It assumes that everything exists in the way it appears—from its own side, with its own inherent nature, independently, able to set itself up, and under its own power. Due to the predispositions of ignorance, phenomena appear to us as discrete, definable, independent entities, and ignorance grasps at them as existing in that way. All these appearances, which are contaminated by our ignorance, are in the nature of suffering. Anything onto which we project inherent existence—whether ourselves or other people, the environment or things around us—is in the nature of suffering. Because we interpolate a false way of existence on them and misapprehend them, they will be unsatisfactory, or dukkha. They're not going to make us everlastingly happy.

Reflecting upon this each morning reminds us that there's no reason to be attached to the people and events we encounter in our lives. Since they are in the nature of suffering, we don't need to be so reactive relating with them. Remembering this cools the mind. Understanding that contaminated phenomena are by nature unsatisfactory doesn't mean we become indifferent and apathetic. Rather, because our mind does not become neurotically involved with people and things, we are able to interact with them with compassion and wisdom, viewing them in a more realistic light.

All phenomena are selfless. All persons and phenomenon—everything that exists, whether it's permanent or impermanent—exists dependently. It is empty of having an independent self. Here, "self" means inherent existence, true existence, existing under its own power. Everything is empty of that impossible way of existence.

When we reflect on this each morning, even briefly, we understand that everything is empty of inherent existence. We then feel that there is space, flexibility, and the possibility for change and growth. When we remember that the things we bump into are not solid, objective entities, we cease to struggle with them. When we remember that everything exists by being merely labeled and not from its own side, we don't get stuck. We realize that phenomena exist like illusions, appearing in one way but existing in another. Thus, our prejudices and preconceptions relax. We cease vacillating between elation and depression.

Nirvana is peace. Nirvana is the cessation of all unsatisfactory conditions (suffering) and their causes. Nirvana is the third Noble Truth, which is the cessation of the first two Noble Truths, the truth of suffering and the truth of the origin of suffering. If we're looking for true peace and happiness, we will aim for nirvana. Rather than thinking that food, sex, recognition, and appreciation bring us happiness, we seek nirvana. Instead of thinking that a new credit card, set of skis, or love affair will fulfill us, we remember that nirvana is real fulfillment. Nirvana—liberation from cyclic existence, the actualization of our potential—is what we aim for each day.

Real peace exists in the mind; it depends on the mind. Lasting peace cannot be legislated or enforced by U.N. peacekeeping forces. While still working to bring about the conditions for external peace—peace on our planet—we must recognize that lasting world peace cannot exist without each and every human being subduing their own ignorance, hostility, and attachment.

Requests and Prayers

Remembering the four seals each morning will help us cultivate our pure spiritual intention. That pure intention on our part is the ring that Tara will hook with her wisdom and compassion. We might ask, "If Tara is a Buddha, why do we have to request her to hook us? Why do we have to request her to guide us and assist us? She became a Buddha to do this. She spent all those eons working to purify her mind and gain all the good qualities of a Buddha. Spontaneously and effortlessly, she manifests to benefit beings, so why do I have to ask her for help?"

We request because when we ask for something, it means that we sincerely want it; we're intent on this. Some years ago my friend was teaching English to one of the little rinpoches in Dharamsala. When the monks in monasteries do a particular puja, they make offerings and repeat requests for inspiration over and over again. One time, they were making 100,000 of these offerings and requests to Guru Rinpoche, Padmasambhava. This little rinpoche asked my friend, "Why do we request the Buddha over and over again 'Please grant me blessings and inspire me'?"

My friend replied, "When you want a snack, do you ask your mother or your teacher once? No, you ask over and over again, don't you?" When we really want something, we don't just ask once and forget it. No, we ask again and again. It's the same thing here. By requesting Tara again and again, "Hook me with your great love and kindness," we're expressing our interest and sincerity. That's part of the equation. The Buddha's actions don't work independently of us. There's a cooperative process, so we have to come forth from our side with our earnestness, our deep wish, and our willingness to engage in the practice. The more open we are, the more the Buddhas and bodhisattvas have something to work with.

An analogy is two bowls, one upside down, the other right-side up. The sun shines indiscriminately on both. But no sunlight can enter the upside-down bowl. Similarly, if our mind is closed and involved with the eight worldly concerns, even if all the Buddhas and bodhisattvas in the universe appeared before us, we would ignore them.

By making these requests, we're taking the upside-down bowl of our mind and trying to turn it right-side up so that the sunlight can fill it. Reciting verses and mantras sincerely and with proper understanding of their meaning makes our mind open and receptive so that the inspiration and teachings of the Buddha can enter and grow.

Tara doesn't need us to ask for her help, but we need to ask for help because we must recognize how important the Dharma is for us. For example, when we want work, we ask for a job over and over again until we get one. We earnestly put a lot of effort into job-hunting because we know the value of getting a paycheck. It's this type of effort and intensity that we have to put into our spiritual practice, too. Just as we view a paycheck, and therefore a job, as important, we need to see our spiritual goals as important and create their causes. In fact, in the long run, they're more important than a job.

Previously, I described Tara as wondrous qualities appearing in the form of a green deity made of light. But in the request prayer, it sounds as if she's an entity, a real person. I believe it's a human tendency to want to see someone outside of ourselves as having special power and ability to do things that we are incapable of doing. There is no fault in seeing Tara as a person, but we must remember she is a non–inherently existent person. As the princess Yeshe Dawa, she was in cyclic existence, practiced the path, and became a Buddha. Similarly, Padmasambhava and Milarepa were ordinary beings like us, practiced the path, and became enlightened. Each of them has a conventional self but is empty of an inherently existent self. The conventional "I" is labeled in dependence on the mindstream, which is also empty of inherent existence. In other words, one mindstream was labeled Padmasambhava for a while, and that mindstream became an enlightened mindstream. Another mindstream was labeled Milarepa for a while, and it, too, became enlightened. But neither of these persons existed inherently. Nor do the Buddhas they became exist inherently. They exist dependent upon causes and conditions, parts, and the mind that conceives and labels them.

Thinking of Buddhas and bodhisattvas as beings can inspire us, because it reminds us that we can become like them. There are different ways of seeing them, and when we see them as beings with a conventional self, it's important to remember that this is an appearance and that they lack inherent existence. They are not external, independent, omnipotent gods who manage the universe.

We can't say, "Tara, please inspire me to develop love and compassion and, in the meantime, I'm going to tell this guy off because he's making so much noise while I'm praying to you." When we request, "Inspire my mind," we're also saying to ourselves, "Having love and compassion is important. I need to make effort from my side to cultivate them."

I once asked His Holiness, "How does requesting the Buddhas to bless and inspire our minds work? Can they inspire and bless us?" His Holiness said that the Buddhas worked very hard to cultivate the path and attain special spiritual qualities that others don't possess, so they should be able to do things that ordinary beings can't. If we visualized President Roosevelt and prayed to him, could he bless and inspire our mind? From his side, has he eliminated all obstacles to benefiting beings? Has he developed full compassion, wisdom, and power? What could Roosevelt, as an ordinary being, actually do for us now?

That made me think. There is a purpose for becoming a Buddha. Someone who has developed unbiased love and compassion toward all beings and who directly perceives the nature of reality has abilities that the rest of us don't. If I don't think that the Buddhas can benefit sentient beings in a myriad of ways, including inspiring their minds, why am I practicing the Dharma in order to become one? I saw that having the bodhichitta motivation meant believing in the four bodies of a Buddha and in their capabilities.

The mind is very powerful. Before I started meditating, I didn't think the mind—including our thoughts and motivations—was so powerful. I believed in the power of physical objects. Once I began to meditate and watch my mind, I learned differently. Have you ever had the experience of your mind being very calm and then suddenly an angry thought comes in? The energy of that angry thought is extremely powerful. Even if nobody else in the room knows about that angry thought, its power and the effect it has upon us is quite strong. We can see that from our own experience.

Sometimes we can sense someone else's negative thoughts. We call it "bad vibes" or "bad energy." They can influence us; they stir up our own unsettled energy and set off our preconceptions and irritation.

Imagine what would happen if we were sensitive to the virtuous thoughts and feelings of a Buddha. That energy would stimulate our wholesome thoughts and feelings and increase them. When we make requests to Tara, we open ourselves up to the energy of her realizations and that can affect us. But if we pray to President Roosevelt, not much will happen because it's unlikely that he had spiritual realizations.

The Tibetan word that is usually translated as "blessing" or "inspiration" can more literally be translated as "to transform into magnificence." We are asking the Buddhas to transform our minds into magnificence. How that happens isn't by the Buddha going in and pulling some switches inside our mind. Because our mind is conditioned and changing, the mental energy of the Buddha's realizations can affect our energy, so to speak. Conditioned phenomena affect each other, so the force of Tara's realizations can positively affect our mind.

Someone told me that he once heard someone request His Holiness the Dalai Lama to pray for world peace. His Holiness commented, "I don't much believe in prayer." How does this relate to the fact that His Holiness makes prayers and requests to Tara?

"Prayer" is not an accurate translation of the Tibetan word *monlam*, which has the connotation of "setting an aspiration." We usually associate praying with asking a supreme being to intercede and change the external conditions of our life, whereas making requests involves generating a strong aspiration or intent on our part. When we do this, we bring forth a virtuous mental state that the Buddhas can influence. We're not asking them to do something for us while we relax and drink tea. We're generating mental states that are beginning to correlate with those of the Buddhas.

When His Holiness says that he doesn't believe in prayer, he's trying to prevent people from thinking that all we have to do is pray for something, but we don't have to take responsibility for making it happen. In Tibetan Buddhism we make long life pujas with elaborate offerings for our teachers. Once some people in the West wanted to do this after a series of teachings, and His Holiness responded, "We don't have time for this. Your praying for my long life won't make me live any longer. But if you sincerely practice the Dharma and subdue your disturbing emotions, that's something worthwhile. That will make me want to live long!"

In terms of how karma works, if we practice the Dharma, the Buddhas and bodhisattvas have a reason to manifest and remain in our world, and our teachers will have long lives. If we don't practice Dharma but just pray for them to live long, there's no purpose for them to be here because we aren't doing anything from our side except blind worship. This is what His Holiness is referring to when he says he doesn't much believe in prayer. We can't simply pray, "May everybody live together peacefully and happily," and then do nothing to make the world a more equitable place. We've got to make world peace happen. How do we make world peace happen? One way is to keep our precepts!

Keeping precepts is the first way to make world peace happen. Second is to generate love and compassion. World peace won't happen by fighting wars to eliminate enemies or by passing laws. There has to be a transformation within each individual. As long as anger exists, irresolvable conflict will exist. Laws can help in certain ways—I'm not saying they're useless, and we need to ensure our society has fair ones—but we can't create world peace through legislation alone when people have anger inside. That's why precepts are so important.

Precepts are wonderful guidelines that the Buddha gave to help us live together in a mutually beneficial way. Abandoning actions such as killing, stealing, lying, unwise sexual behavior, and intoxicants seems so obvious. We learned this in Sunday school as kids. It's so important to avoid these negativities, yet many people regularly engage in them. When we live in precepts, everyone who encounters us will feel safe. They know that we won't harm them physically, take their things, or manipulate them through distorting the truth. Keeping precepts is one way we can personally contribute to world peace. We may think that one individual abiding in precepts doesn't make much change, but just think what the world would be like if Adolph Hitler had kept precepts. Just think what the newspaper headlines would be if everyone kept the first precept not to kill for one day!

VERSE 2: CONNECTING WITH TARA

By the witness of the Three Jewels, not just from my mouth but from the depths of my innermost heart and bones, I pray to you morning and evening. Show your blissful face to me, Loving One. Grant me the nectar of your speech.

"By the witness of the Three Jewels" means we're asking the Buddha, Dharma, and Sangha to witness what we're saying. Since we respect the Three Jewels, we won't lie or chatter idly; we'll say something that is well thought out and in earnest. "Not just from my mouth" means not insincerely "but from the very depths of my innermost heart and bones." Isn't that a wonderful image?

"I pray to you morning and evening." We could take this literally if it helps us to set aside a specific time of the day to practice. However, let's aim to develop an attitude in which Tara and her outstanding qualities are in our hearts all the time, not just in the morning and evening.

"Show your blissful face to me, Loving One. Grant me the nectar of your speech." It sounds as if we are asking Tara to walk in the door so we can see her face. What is Tara's face? What does seeing Tara mean? The Buddha said, "Those who see the Dharma see me." Seeing the Dharma means realizing emptiness, realizing the way in which things exist, their deepest mode of existence. When we have actualized the wisdom that realizes emptiness, we know what the Buddha is and what Tara is. Seeing Tara doesn't mean having a vision of Tara. It means accessing the way that things exist by understanding emptiness. Seeing Tara involves experiencing the same wisdom that is her nature.

People have all kinds of experiences in meditation. A friend once told me that he spoke with a Tibetan monk meditating above Dharamsala. This monk mentioned that he had just had a vision of Tara. My friend got very excited and said, "Was it Tara? What did she say? What happened?" The monk was very nonchalant and said, "I don't know if it was Tara," as if it didn't matter.

In other words, if you have a vision and it inspires you in your practice because you feel close to the Buddha, that's beneficial. If you have a vision and get attached to it, thinking that now you're someone special, that's opposite to the Dharma. Whether the vision actually was Tara or not doesn't matter. What's more important is how we relate to the vision. If we have an insight in meditation and use it to bolster our ego, it was useless. If we have only an approximate insight but use it to increase our enthusiasm for practice, it was useful.

People can have all sorts of wonderful experiences in meditation and become attached to those experiences. Some people try to recreate these experiences in future meditation sessions, which usually leads to frustration. Or, sometimes they create an identity about them. They tell many people what they experienced, as if to imply they're special. Doing this causes the experience to degenerate; it becomes a lovely memory of something long gone. Dreams are similar. We can interpret them in many different ways. It isn't as if a dream has one meaning and we've got to get that one meaning. Dreams are not good or bad from their own side. More important is how we relate to the dream and what we learn from it.

Before highest yoga tantra initiations, the lama passes out *kusha* grass and instructs the disciples to observe their dreams that night. The next day, people are so excited, "What did you dream? This is what I dreamt...!" They think it's something special. Then, the lama describes indicators of auspicious dreams, and some people get more excited. Then, the lama says, "But they're only dreams. They don't exist from their own side. They don't exist as they appear," and people sigh with disappointment, "My special dream was only a dream. What a pity!" We observe our dreams the night before initiation because dreams are used as an analogy for the illusory nature of phenomena that are empty by nature. The people who got so excited missed that point entirely.

"Show your blissful face to me, Loving One" is an appeal to our own wisdom: "May I perceive emptiness." Tara's blissful face is the face of emptiness.

"Grant me the nectar of your speech." They say that the way the Buddha helps us the most is through teaching the Dharma, that the speech of the Buddha is what is most important to us sentient beings. Among the body, speech, and mind of the Buddha, which do you think is most significant for us? One person might say the Buddha's mind because that is his realizations; another might say the Buddha's body because she would like to have a vision of it. But neither of these is the most important aspect for us sentient beings. A Buddha's speech is most crucial for us, because the Buddha leads us on the path to enlightenment by teaching the Dharma. Without the teachings, we wouldn't know what to practice and what to abandon on the path. That's why it's important to request teachings by sincerely reciting the seven-limb prayer and by directly asking our spiritual mentor for teachings. Similarly, when Dharma groups invite teachers to come, they should write sincere letters of invitation. That shows they're earnest. We need to request teachings from our hearts because we know how important it is to hear the Dharma. This is why the Buddha's speech is more important for us than his body or mind.

One time, a center in North Carolina invited me to teach. They made the initial contact and arrangements by email, and then they wrote a very nice letter confirming the date and saying, "We're looking forward to having you come. We'd like you to teach this. You'll see that our center has grown and changed since you were last here." I appreciated their letter, not because I needed the affirmation, but because it showed that these people were conscientious and sincere.

Verse 3: Spiritual Mentors

Great gurus and small gurus cheat us with their made-up teachings, selling Dharma, teaching without comprehension, not observing who is qualified and who is not, being concerned about their own happiness and the eight worldly concerns. Since I can no longer trust friends of this degenerate age, you are my principal guru. Inspire me, Divine Mother, essence of love. Arouse the great power of your compassion and think of me.

We live in an age of degeneration, a time in which people have strong and persistent disturbing attitudes and negative emotions and hold stubbornly to inaccurate views. Since this is the case, we have to be attentive and responsible when selecting spiritual mentors, for not everyone who is promoted as a spiritual teacher is necessarily a qualified one. Lamrim texts explain the qualities we should look for in excellent spiritual mentors. For example, qualified teachers live in pure ethical discipline, have developed some meditative concentration, and have some insight into emptiness. We should look for mentors who teach with genuine concern for the disciples' spiritual well-being, not those who seek fame, offerings, and a retinue of disciples. Our teachers should have extensive and profound understanding of the Dharma and be able to teach many topics and practices. Furthermore, we want teachers who are extremely patient and tolerant because we aren't always the best students. The importance of examining someone over time before taking him or her as our spiritual mentor cannot be emphasized enough, especially in the age of the spiritual supermarket. It is our responsibility to examine people before considering them our spiritual teachers in order to see if they have some or all of the above qualities. Instead of being emotional and impulsive, let's choose our spiritual teachers wisely and not rush into things.

I think that "great gurus" refers to famous teachers and "small gurus" to those who aren't as well known. People can be very famous and have a large following, but that doesn't mean they have profound comprehension of the Dharma or are qualified teachers. Following a particular teacher simply because he or she is the latest rage is not a good reason. Those who are actually great gurus—that is, those who have correct realizations—are not involved in the eight worldly concerns and are always humble.

Famous gurus and not-so-famous gurus can "cheat us with their made-up teachings." Some people mix non-Buddhist teachings with Buddhist practices and call it Buddhism. Others misunderstand the Buddha's teachings but don't realize that they've misunderstood it, and teach their misunderstanding as if it were what the Buddha taught. Some people have a spectacular dream or an unusual experience in meditation and think they have attained high realizations. Some of them create their own spiritual tradition; New Age newsletters are full of this. There you can find any kind of belief system you want, all of which are guaranteed to bring you quickly to enlightenment—for a small fee.

For students interested in Buddhadharma, "made-up teachings" are those that lack a lineage back to the Buddha. We want to study with teachers who have received teachings from a qualified teacher who received his or her training from another qualified teacher, all the way back to the Buddha. This is one way to ensure that we receive valid teachings.

Why is it important to receive authentic teachings from a qualified spiritual mentor? Because these are the teachings we will practice. If we learn an incorrect path, we will practice an incorrect path and won't progress spiritually. Even if we put a lot of time and energy into practicing those teachings, our efforts will be wasted because the practices aren't based on the correct view. It's comparable to cooking with a bad cookbook. We may sincerely want to cook a good meal and may spend all day doing it, but if the recipes we follow are bad, we'll end up with something inedible.

Following someone who has made up teachings or "modernized" the teachings in a way that makes them more palatable for our ego is dangerous. For example, someone may say, "Buddha didn't teach a complete path to enlightenment. You also need psychotherapy to get enlightened," or "You only have to do one practice to attain enlightenment, and coincidentally, it is the one that I teach," or "Thinking about selflessness makes you uncomfortable? Just leave it. It's not important for enlightenment."

Sometimes devious people make things up, but more often, people don't have a conscious bad intention. They're just misinformed and don't know the Dharma well. Others may know the Dharma well, but gripped by arrogance, they don't realize that they're not the advanced practitioners they think they are. I heard a story of a Dharma student who thought her teacher had started speaking through her. It seems this person had some mental difficulties, but nobody was able to get through to her. She was convinced that she was channeling her guru who had passed away. She began teaching and was apparently charismatic, but then became psychologically manipulative, which left the students confused.

In thinking of the potential corruptions great gurus and small gurus could fall prey to, we might be tempted to start judging our teachers. "This guru does this, that guru does that, but *I'm* very pure. *I* would never do any of these things." We feel superior and look down on our spiritual mentors with contempt. This way of thinking is a huge obstacle in our practice.

We must remember that this verse isn't just talking about what other people do. It is also talking about us, about our own propensity to make up teachings, our propensity to sell the Dharma and use the Dharma to make money. So let's not to use this verse as an excuse to be more critical of others. We already have enough contempt and judgment. We don't need excuses to practice those!

"Teaching without comprehension"—that is, not understanding a topic but teaching it anyway—is a great way to create lots of negative karma. Teaching without comprehension is dangerous, for we can easily lead others astray. This is easy to do, because we don't always realize that we don't understand. We may think that because we've read a book or a transcript and understand something at one level, that we've understood it completely.

Then, to cover up our ignorance when people ask questions we can't respond to, we may make up answers, humiliate the person who asks the question, or change the topic. This helps neither the other nor ourselves. Whether we're teaching the Dharma formally or just answering a friend's question, we need to be honest and say, "I don't know," when we don't know.

There is nothing wrong with saying that. Nobody expects us to know everything. We simply say, "I don't know, but I'll read up on it and ask others who know more than me," or "Let me think about that some more and get back to you later." There's no reason to be ashamed if we reply in that way. Saying we don't know rather than feigning we do is a sign of integrity.

In my own practice, the more I go over the beginning Lamrim topics such as precious human life, the more layers of meaning I discover in them. If there are so many layers of meaning in a topic found at the beginning of the path, of course there will be even more profundity to discover in more advanced topics.

Dana—Generosity

This verse speaks of selling the Dharma, a topic about which I feel strongly. Traditionally, Dharma teachings have been open to everybody regardless of whether they have money or not. Dharma shouldn't be just for people with a certain income level. Since everyone can benefit from the Dharma, everyone should be able to hear it.

In the West where it's often difficult for Dharma centers to stay afloat financially, many of them charge for teachings. In Asia, people understand *dana* and giving offerings. They know that they create great positive potential by giving, and they want to make the teachings available to others. But in the West, if a price isn't charged, people think it's not worth anything. And if you ask for donations, they think two dollars is enough. As a result, many centers and/or teachers charge for teachings and initiations to cover costs. I can understand why they do this, but it makes me uncomfortable. First, people don't create positive potential and fail to develop the quality of generosity, both of which are essential to progress on the path. When we make a donation, we create positive potential. When we pay a fee, we don't. Second, people see themselves as consumers, not as spiritual students. In the market economy, the consumer demands and the supplier supplies. But that isn't a healthy type of relationship between a student (consumer) and their spiritual mentor (supplier).

In the case of a retreat, the organizers have to rent the retreat center and buy food. It's fair to charge for that, although I would like to see even that offered on dana basis. But in my opinion, the teachings must be given freely. Let's give people a chance to open their hearts in generosity and free themselves from the mind that constantly says, "What will I get out of this?"

Personally speaking, I've decided to live on dana. I don't want to get paid for teaching, counseling, or writing. I give freely, and hopefully people will reciprocate. They know I need food, shelter, clothing, and medicine. I believe Dharma teachers, and especially monastics, should live simply. We're supposed to be practicing the three principal aspects of the path, the first of which is renunciation. Why should we drive new cars, live in luxurious houses, go on expensive vacations, and wear fashionable clothing?

The Dharma is not a commodity for sale. At the end of His Holiness the Dalai Lama's teachings in San Jose in 2002, the organizers announced how much profit had been made from the teachings and to whom they would donate the money. The causes to which they were donating were excellent. But after a similar thing happened at his next teaching in Los Angeles, His Holiness said, "My teachings should not be venues for fund-raising. Rather than charging a lot and giving the money away, you could make the tickets cheaper so that they just cover the costs of organizing the event. That way, more people who don't have a lot of money can attend."

Many times, people simply don't know what a Dharma center's expenses are, and so they don't think to give. For example, at Dharma Friendship Foundation, the center in Seattle where I taught for ten years, the group's expenses included rent for the center, utilities, publicity, bookshelves, cushions, and the teacher's food, rent, and health insurance. But unless people were charged or asked directly for money, it seems many of them didn't consider from where the money came to meet these expenses.

People in the West also need to be educated so that they understand the purpose and value of generosity. Dana entails being generous because we care and take delight in giving. Dana is not just a fancy or polite name for paying. For example, at the conclusion of a teaching or retreat the organizers often give a "dana talk" to encourage people to give. But people are so used to paying that they then think, "What would be a reasonable charge for what I've received? That's how much dana I will give." This is not a suitable way to be generous because the mind is still thinking of payment for services. Some people dislike being challenged to give from the heart and get stuck thinking, "What is a fair price for this? Even though they haven't told me, I'll figure it out, and that's how much I'll give." That attitude isn't generosity. When teaching about generosity, the first of the six far-reaching attitudes, the Buddha talked about taking delight in giving. Generosity is a mind that takes joy in giving, a mind that wants to give, a mind that sees something virtuous and wants to support it.

Whether we give a dollar or a million dollars isn't important. The important thing is that we want to support what is virtuous and feel joy in doing so. The mind takes delight in sharing what we have. We're not thinking in terms of numbers and "what is fair," but instead are happy to share. Such a wonderful attitude is the cause of happiness for ourselves and others.

Because many people don't have the mentality of generosity, then organizers, Dharma centers, or teachers find themselves in the position of charging fees for the Dharma because they need money to cover costs. But, let's say we re-educate our minds so that we take delight in helping the Dharma to exist and spread. Then, with a group of friends, we make a donation to cover the costs of an upcoming teaching. At that time, we might say to the organizers, "Let's make this teaching available for as many people as possible, free of charge." Then the organizers won't have to charge for Dharma events. Teachings in Asia are organized in this way, and the joy is infectious. Whenever I attend teachings there, I think of the kindness of the benefactors and dedicate for their well-being and enlightenment. Their generosity inspires me to practice.

Those in the position of a Dharma teacher must take care not to sell the Dharma. To me, this includes not teaching in order to earn their livelihood. If they do, teaching the Dharma becomes like a job, and of course, people want to be paid well for their work. Traditionally, Dharma teachers have not charged, because most of them were monastics. Monastics live simply; they don't need to support a family. They wear the same clothes every day, don't use jewelry or cosmetics, don't listen to music or go out for entertainment. The Buddhist community was grateful to have people keeping pure ethical discipline nearby and voluntarily gave them food, shelter, clothing, and medicine. Thus, the monastics were free to study, practice, and teach and didn't have to think about how to get their next meal.

The situation today is very different. Many Buddhist teachers are lay people who have a family to support. They need a house for their kids. They need a car, furniture, clothes, jewelry, magazine subscriptions, CD players, bicycles, and so on. They want their children to fit in with everyone else, so they need all the things that middle-class people have. The question then arises, "Is it the responsibility of the Dharma students to pay for the teacher's kids to have new Nike shoes? To pay for the teacher's spouse to go to the gym to exercise? To cover the mortgage on the teacher's house?" These are new questions that arise due to having lay Dharma teachers with a middle-class lifestyle. Both students and teachers need to give some serious thought to these questions.

A person may be a sincere practitioner and just want to teach and practice. But if they also have to cover the costs of a middle class lifestyle and support their family they may begin to consider how much dana they get when they teach. They may decide which people to teach or which centers to go to based on how much they get from teaching there. That can distort their motivation, and that of the students as well. Students might seek to receive special attention by giving a lot of money to the teacher, and the teacher might give that attention because they need the income.

"Not observing who is qualified and who is not." Teachers need to observe which disciples are qualified before they teach them. Students need to be qualified disciples to benefit from the level of teachings being given. But sometimes in order to gain a lot of followers, teachers may indiscriminately teach whatever they think the students want to hear. Nowadays, many people want the highest, most exotic teachings—highest yoga tantra, dzogchen, and mahamudra—and that's what we request our spiritual mentors to teach. Tibetan teachers figure that it will plant good seeds in the students' minds to hear such teachings. So they give these very advanced teachings, and having heard some fantastic words and concepts, we think that we've understood them. Then, when we hear instructions such as "Taking intoxicants is harmful" or "Attachment causes suffering," we get upset. We don't want to hear basic teachings on ethical discipline that interfere with our pleasure. "Why are you telling me to stop drinking? That has nothing to do with my spiritual practice. I'm meditating on this high practice." Such an attitude is a fault in the student.

A teacher with unclear motivations may give teachings that students aren't yet sufficiently prepared to hear. Other teachers give advanced teachings out of compassion, because they want to plant good seeds in the students' minds. But students do not always appreciate this. We want to take initiations, but we don't want to keep the vows or do a daily practice. Or, if we do the practice daily, we want to do the shortest version. If we expect teachers to be deeply engaged with us, we have to make ourselves into better qualified disciples by improving our own capabilities so that we become more receptive vessels. Then, naturally, teachers will fill that vessel with teachings.

Becoming a Qualified Student

How do we become a qualified disciple? One quality to develop is open-mindedness. In other words, we let go of our own hard and fast agenda, of our likes and dislikes, and of our erroneous opinions about the nature of reality or the stages of the path. If we attend a teaching yet still hold strongly to our preconceptions about the path, we will evaluate teachers by whether or not they agree with our ideas. Is that a valid criterion for selecting a teacher? Such an attitude blocks us from learning because we're holding on to what we believe and only accepting what validates our own opinions. In that case, we aren't receptive to the Enlightened One's teachings. To learn, we must set aside our own prejudices, be open-minded, and listen with a fresh mind.

The second quality of an excellent disciple is intelligence. This isn't referring to a person's IQ, because people with high IQs can be dull when it comes to understanding the Dharma. Intelligence means a willingness to investigate the teachings and think about them. We don't just accept things on face value, "Yes, the teacher said it, therefore it's true." Rather, we think about things, examine them using reason, and apply them to our own experiences. A disciple with this quality is willing to do the work of deeply investigating the meaning of the teachings.

The third quality is earnestness or sincerity, that is, a pure motivation.

Having a pure motivation at the beginning of our practice is difficult. It takes time to develop it; we start with the earnestness, sincerity, and genuine spiritual longing that we have now, and then we build upon them.

Some people automatically think they have a pure motivation and are intelligent and open-minded. How can we be a good spiritual disciple if we already think we are one? That's arrogance. On the other hand, let's not go to the other extreme of low self-esteem, "I'm totally unqualified. My nose is in the mud. I can't learn anything." That's also ridiculous. Let's try to have a realistic appraisal of ourselves that enables us to be both humble and confident. "I've developed some qualities, and there's a long way to go." Humility is based on self-confidence but leaves us open to learning, whereas arrogance closes the door to learning.

We come to the Dharma with a wide variety of motivations. We don't start with bodhichitta, do we? How many of us have actual, spontaneous bodhichitta? Maybe you do; I don't. I have a hard enough time generating effortful, fabricated bodhichitta, which is the kind that we develop when we consciously cultivate our motivation. We have to be honest here and acknowledge our selfish motivations. This honesty is a sign of integrity in our spiritual practice; it enables us to develop better and better qualities.

Vigilantly observing and continuously cultivating our motivation is important, because after we've been around for a while, sneaky motivations can creep in. "I want to learn the Dharma so I can teach it to others." This could translate into, "…and then I'll have a good position in the group and people will appreciate and respect me." We have to check our motivations for wanting to teach Dharma. "I'll learn the Dharma so that I can write things and people will think that I'm knowledgeable and spiritual. I'll learn the Dharma so I can be close to my teachers, and then they'll fulfill my emotional needs." Various misguided motivations may easily creep in.

We can be truthful about what's going on in our minds without falling into low self-esteem and self-hatred. Let's be honest that, until we become Buddhas, there will always be ways to grow. That humility keeps us open. His Holiness the Dalai Lama exemplifies humility, and he's certainly more advanced on the path than we are. So if somebody more advanced than us can humbly admit, "I don't fully understand the great texts," shouldn't we also have a modicum of humility? There's nothing wrong with not knowing everything!

"Not observing who is qualified and who is not." I remember in the mid-seventies when people were just learning Tibetan Buddhism, they would often request highest yoga tantra initiations from Lama Yeshe, "Lama, please give us Yamantaka and Heruka initiations." Lama Yeshe would shoo them out, saying, "Go meditate on Lamrim and thought transformation. Learn to be kind to each other first."

The Eight Worldly Concerns

"Being concerned about their own happiness and the eight worldly concerns." This refers to teachers who are concerned about their own comfort, reputation, approval, status, possessions, or finances. When we are principally concerned with our own well-being in the world, it's difficult to be good teachers for others. The more we are concerned about the happiness of others, the better teachers we become, because we'll be more concerned about the students' development than with patting ourselves on the back for being a good teacher: "How wonderful I am! I helped this person learn the Dharma. I have so many devoted students and they follow me around. They praise me and recite my long life prayer." Or, "Look what my students bought! They offered me this and that. Let me show you..." It's very easy for ego to do this dance.

But it's not only the big gurus and small gurus who are involved in the eight worldly concerns. Let's be inclusive and non-biased and talk about ourselves as well! There are four pairs of worldly concerns, making eight altogether:

1. feeling happy when we receive material possessions and money and unhappy when we don't;
2. being pleased when we are praised and people approve of us and depressed when they disapprove of us or criticize us;
3. feeling elated when we have a good reputation or image and horrified when we don't; and

4. being delighted when we have sense pleasures and miserable when we don't.

Happiness at having possessions, praise, reputation, or sense pleasures easily leads us to being attached to them, and that attachment causes many problems. What is a healthy relationship to have with money? Having money is not a problem, neither is earning money. We don't need to feel guilty for having money. We need money to function in society. However, problems arise when we cling to the money, when we are attached to possessions, when we think that money symbolizes success, love, power, and freedom.

Having and not having material possessions and financial wealth. Our drawers, closets, attics, and basements are stuffed to the gills. If we're lucky, we'll clean them out before Christmas to make room for new Christmas presents. How reluctant we can be to give things away! One time, I gave students at Dharma Friendship Foundation the homework assignment to give things away. First, they had to do something simple, such as clean out a closet and give away unwanted things. The next week, they had to give away something they liked. This homework assignment wound up lasting for several weeks because the first week, many people didn't do it. They needed to be reminded and given another chance. By the following week some people had moved the unwanted things as far as the front door or the trunk of their car. They still hadn't actually given them to others.

Examining our attachment to material things can be eye-opening. Often we aren't aware of how we hoard things and of how difficult it is to part with possessions, even if they're ones we seldom use. But if we want to practice the bodhisattva path and far-reaching generosity, we need to overcome the eight worldly concerns in order to continuously increase our delight in giving.

When I moved from Seattle, some of my things were given to different people in DFF. Later, when I visited some students, it was like a flashback. "There's my dish. There's my quilt." I had to remind myself, "No they're not mine anymore. That label doesn't belong on them now. They belong to somebody else." It was interesting for me to see that even after giving them away, the label "mine" was still on them.

Feeling miserable when we don't get material possessions or money occurs, for example, when we think somebody should give us a present and they don't, or when we don't get the things that we want. When somebody else has nicer shoes, a more expensive car, a better apartment, a more comfortable sofa, and so on, our mind desires these things and we're unhappy because we don't have them. This unhappiness and discontent arises due to our attachment. The problem isn't having or not having the things; the real problem is having the attachment that precipitates fear of not getting what we want or of losing what we have. Due to attachment, anger arises when our possessions and money are jeopardized.

In Dharma class we may feel so renounced. "I can give everything away. I'm not attached." But when we leave the teaching and can't find our shoes, we growl, "Who took my shoes?" We get angry when something simple, like our shoes, disappears.

I love the story of the Buddha asking a stingy person to give a carrot from one hand to the other. Sometimes we can practice giving from the right hand to the left and back again. Then, we can try putting the carrot into somebody else's hand. A hand is a hand; it doesn't matter whether it's ours or somebody else's. It's the giving that's important.

Receiving praise and blame. The second pair is being attached to approval, appreciation, and praise. This one is much more insidious than attachment to money and material possessions. We want our family to approve of us; we want our friends to approve of us. When our friends don't approve of us, we get shaky. For example, when we first become a Buddhist and our old friends ask, "What in the world are you doing?" we begin to doubt, "Well, what in the world am I doing? Why should I go to Dharma class? I should go partying with them." Even though people tell their children, "Don't succumb to peer pressure," they certainly do. When friends don't approve of what we do, we're tempted to relinquish our own values and do what they want.

We adore praise. We feel we deserve it. The world is usually pretty mean and doesn't give us enough praise, does it? We don't necessarily practice praising other people, but we certainly feel they should compliment us because, after all, look how much we've done, how much we've given, how magnanimous we are. People should praise us, or if they don't praise us to our face, at least they should appreciate us. Don't you think so? We're quite attached to this kind of reinforcement and often become insecure, indignant, or full of self-pity when we don't get it.

When we are blamed, our ego feels under attack. The notion of "I" comes up strongly, and we fume, "How dare they say that about *me!*" The problem isn't whether we receive approval and praise, or whether we receive disapproval and blame. The problem is our attachment to the former and aversion to the latter. We often think that who we are depends on what other people think about us.

When we look for reinforcement from others, we don't develop the ability to evaluate ourselves realistically. Let's train ourselves to be able to look inside, see our own faults without hating ourselves, and see our good qualities without being arrogant. With practice, we can develop the ability to understand our motivations and purify them so that we aren't as dependent on other people to reflect back to us whether what we're doing is okay or not. If we do something with a good motivation and we're clear about it, then even if others criticize, there's no reason for us to be upset or to doubt ourselves. On the other hand, if we act with a shady motivation, then even if our action seems benevolent and others praise us, we need to purify.

In addition, it's necessary to develop the ability to evaluate our own actions and motivations so that we don't develop an identity based only on what other people think about us. Other people are very contradictory in their opinions. They see us through the veils of their own needs and preconceptions.

However, learning to evaluate ourselves doesn't mean we just ignore others' feedback. Our Dharma friends have a different perspective from ordinary people and can point out things to us that others wouldn't. Paying heed to Dharma friends helps our practice. Further, if our teacher says something, we should take it to heart and check our mind. A true practitioner welcomes wise advice from others, even if it's not what their self-centered attitude wants to hear.

Having a good reputation and image and having bad ones. We usually feel happy when we have a good reputation and despair when we don't. Reputation and image are what a group of people thinks about us. Whatever our profession is, we want everyone in that profession to think that we're good. In our family, we want to be seen as successful. Whatever our hobby, we want others to know that we excel in it. Not only politicians and movie stars hunger for fame and reputation; we do, too! We each have our own little domains in which we want to have a good reputation. With attachment, we take great care to create a good image. When someone criticizes us behind our back or trashes us, we go ballistic, don't we? When someone in our workplace ruins our reputation...UGH! Some people even commit suicide when their reputation gets ruined. The disadvantages of the eight worldly concerns are readily apparent. They bring so much suffering now and impel us to do negative actions that bring us misery in the future.

When practicing the bodhisattva path, it's useful to have a good reputation because others' confidence in us enables us to benefit them. If we do things that cause other people to lose respect for us, benefiting them and teaching them the Dharma will be difficult. If others don't trust us, it will hard to help them. So out of care for them, we act properly. This is entirely different from being attached to our reputation and pretending to be something that we're not. One is being trustworthy, the other is being deceptive.

Two mental factors come into play here: pretension and deceit. Pretension is pretending that we have good qualities that we don't have, and deceit is pretending we don't have bad qualities that we do have. We are very good at this, aren't we? We are expert on how to precisely phrase something to make it sound as if we had a pure motivation and are very compassionate. We adeptly pretend that we don't have a certain fault that everybody knows we have, "Who me? Why, I would never do that!"

Having pleasant and unpleasant sensual experiences. We like and then get attached to pleasurable experiences, and we dislike and become hostile toward disagreeable ones. We are attracted by pleasant things to see—scenery, a house, a painting, an attractive person—and things to hear—nice music, chimes. We like fragrant smells, delicious tastes, and comfortable tactile experiences. We are unhappy when we don't get these things or when we experience unpleasant ones. Much of our anger originates here. For example, if we're uncomfortable when we travel, we get angry. When we have to listen to obnoxious music, we get upset. When we order food at a restaurant and it doesn't taste the way we think it should, we scold the waiter. The greater our attachment to having pleasant sensual experiences, the greater our anger when we experience unpleasant sensations.

Equanimity and contentment regarding the objects of the eight worldly concerns make our minds calmer and our actions more considerate. We can practice thinking, "Whatever money and possessions I have are good enough." That doesn't mean we don't work to have more in the future. But we don't do so with the attitude that "I've *got* to have this or else I'm going to be miserable." We can still acquire things we need, but with a different motivation.

Think, "The amount of praise and appreciation I receive is sufficient. I'm content with it." Imagine being content with the amount of love and appreciation you receive. Try to let go of the needy, dissatisfied mind that clings to wanting more. Say to yourself and imagine feeling, "However much people love me is good enough. However much people appreciate me is good enough. However much they praise me is good enough. I have my own internal sense of well-being. There's a lot of love inside, and I'm going to focus on sharing that with others." Training our mind to think like this is real Dharma practice.

Think, "Whatever my reputation, it is good enough." What's the advantage of having a good reputation and being well known, anyway? A good reputation won't keep us from a lower rebirth. It won't get us closer to enlightenment. It won't increase our wisdom and compassion. It won't solve starvation and conflicts in the world. So why should we be so intent on having a good reputation and be so tremendously upset when we don't? In terms of worldly things, try to be content, "What I am is good enough; what I have is good enough; my rank at work is good enough. The food they serve at the retreat is good enough. The temperature in the room is good enough."

Once, one person wrote on the feedback form after a retreat, "The food here is too good. It should be simpler because I'm overeating and then I get sleepy in meditation." The next person wrote, "There is too much processed food here, which is not very healthy. They should serve better food." Totally opposite feedback! The temperature in the meditation hall is too hot for one person and too cold for another. One person wants the window open, the other doesn't. Does being in Tara's pure land mean you get to decide on the temperature? Or does it mean that your mind is happy whatever the temperature is?

The more we generate an attitude of contentment in our lives, the happier we will be and the more open we will be to engage in genuine Dharma practice. Letting go of the eight worldly concerns brings mental peace right now.

The defining characteristic of a thought or action being Dharma is whether or not we're attached to the happiness of this life. These eight worldly concerns are completely involved with attachment to the happiness of this life. How can we practice genuine Dharma when our self-centered mind is fixated on getting our own way and making everyone and everything around us suit our preferences and needs?

That doesn't mean the happiness of this life is bad or wrong. The Buddha did not say that we should suffer in this life so that we'll get our reward in heaven. The objects we're attached to and have aversion for aren't the problem; there's nothing wrong with experiencing pleasure and happiness. Those aren't the issue. Rather, attachment to pleasant feelings and to the people, objects, and situations that cause them, and aversion to unpleasant ones—it is these emotions that create trouble. They make us unhappy and propel us to harm others in order to get what we want. The troublemakers of attachment and hostility are what we want to abandon, not people and things. There is nothing wrong with being happy. But when we're attached to it, we actually create more unhappiness for ourselves.

When we're attached to very limited happiness—my own happiness now, to be precise—practicing Dharma becomes difficult because all our time and energy go into procuring the things that give us pleasure. Even when we try to practice Dharma, our motivation is easily polluted by seeking to receive offerings, respect, status, or approval. To the extent that we are involved in the eight worldly concerns, our motivation is corrupted, even when we're trying to practice virtue.

Avoid going to the extreme of thinking, "I have all eight worldly concerns and probably a few more, so I can't practice Dharma. It's impossible.

Everything I do is selfish, so why try?" That is not the proper conclusion. There's no benefit in blaming or hating ourselves because our mind is entranced by the eight worldly concerns. Rather, let's be aware that our mind makes us miserable when it is entrapped by these emotions. On one hand, Dharma practice is the process of letting go of these eight; on the other, true Dharma practice begins when we let go of these eight. Because we want to be happy, let's practice letting go of these eight.

Our Dharma practice is frequently a mixture of worldly concern and Dharma aspiration, isn't it? We work for future lives, liberation, and enlightenment, and we also seek some benefit in this lifetime. Attachment to that benefit pollutes our motivation. If, in this life, we benefit from activities but we're not attached to them, our motivation remains pure. For example, His Holiness the Dalai Lama receives many offerings when he teaches. He uses some and gives the rest away to support the Tibetan government-in-exile, Tibetan monasteries and nunneries, hospitals, relief organizations, and other worthwhile projects. He recently gave the nuns in Mundgod, India, money for a new debating ground because they don't receive as many offerings as the monks. His Holiness doesn't live in a lush, expensive house with a hot tub and a swimming pool. He's content with a simple life. He wears the same clothes every day and is happy. Imagine that!

Meditating on death and impermanence is an excellent antidote to the eight worldly concerns. Write this in big letters in your notebook. Use your yellow pen to highlight it. When we're involved with the eight worldly concerns, our view of life and of our potential is very narrow. We feel that we will live forever and that this life is all there is. We get stuck in that limited view. When we think, "I'm going to die and leave this body, leave this ego-identity, leave all the people around me who help me construct this identity," then we start to ask ourselves, "Considering that one day I will die, what's important at the time of death?" Not our possessions; they can't come with us. Not praise and appreciation, because everybody here may praise us, but it doesn't do us much good when we're dying. Having a good reputation doesn't help us when we're dying. Past sense pleasures are also of no use to us at that time.

What's important is the amount of practice we've done, the internal transformation, the extent to which we've developed good qualities and planted good karmic seeds in our mind. These influence how we die, where we're reborn, and our ability to practice and to gain realizations in future lives. So if our Dharma practice is important at the time of death and in future lives, we should put energy into it now.

Whether we make an extra five dollars, whether we have spaghetti sauce with or without vegetables, whether our car has a dent in it or not, whether everybody at the office thinks we're wonderful or not—none of that is very important because it's temporary; it doesn't last long. At the time of death, do we want to be thinking about our daily worries and cravings? If not, then why let them overwhelm our mind when we're alive?

The meditation on death is excellent because it helps us set our priorities. When our priorities are clear, we live a life without confusion because we know what we want to do and we go about doing it. Our mortality makes it evident that caring for and cultivating our mind/heart is most important. Of course, we do what is necessary to keep our body alive and healthy, but our attention is principally focused on our mind. We work to develop good qualities and engage in constructive actions. We try to transform our minds and hearts into the path to enlightenment.

The meditation on death and impermanence isn't done to make us depressed; it actually frees us from much of the pain of this life because it puts things into perspective. We can see that so many of the things we get depressed or upset about just aren't that important and we let them go.

Let's return to the verse. Saying "I can no longer trust friends of this degenerate age" does not mean we can't trust our spiritual teachers. We *must* trust our spiritual mentors. But we should also choose them wisely. Just because somebody is a spiritual teacher doesn't mean she must be *our* spiritual teacher. Just because somebody has many students doesn't mean that we must also be *their student*. As responsible students, we examine potential teachers and get to know them. After seeing that they have the qualities to be good spiritual guides, we may take them as our teachers. But once we've accepted them as our teachers, we should trust them. If we don't trust them, it will be difficult to progress spiritually because when they give us Dharma advice, we will constantly be resistant and doubt their wisdom. Of course, if a teacher gives us Dharma advice that is against the general Buddhist teachings, we should not follow it. We always need to use discriminating wisdom. But if a teacher instructs us according to the scriptures and gives us good advice, even if they say something that impinges on our ego's pleasure, we should be open and take it to heart.

I recommend Alex Berzin's *Relating to a Spiritual Teacher*. It will give you some insight about how to select and relate to spiritual teachers. It also describes how to become a more qualified disciple.

When we say to Tara, "you are my principal guru," it means that the wisdom of the Buddha is our principal guru. "Inspire me, Divine Mother, essence of love. Arouse the great power of your compassion and think of me." Here, we ask Tara for her help and inspiration. We also say to ourselves, "I'm making myself ready to receive the enlightening influence of Tara and of all the Buddhas. I want to follow the path and do the meditations necessary to develop those qualities."

VERSE 4: MEDITATION DEITIES

> *I take refuge in you, Tara; like you, no Buddha could ever deceive me. But understanding the odd character of these times, most Buddhas have gone into the bliss of nirvana. Even though they have great compassion, we have no connection. Since for me there are no other deities, you are my principal deity. Bestow realizations upon me, Divine Mother, essence of love. Arouse the great power of your compassion and think of me.*

The previous verse concerned how to relate to gurus. This verse is about how to relate to Buddhas and meditation deities (*yidams*). The following verse concerns our relationship with protectors. These are the principal relationships we have with realized beings when we practice.

"No Buddha could ever deceive us." Buddhas have eliminated all defilements from their mindstreams. They are totally free from selfishness and thus have no motivation to deceive us. Since they are free from ignorance, they can't mislead us.

"Understanding the odd character of these times, most Buddhas have gone into the bliss of nirvana" means that we live in a degenerate age where sentient beings don't have much positive potential, or merit. When sentient beings don't practice, when they lack positive potential, then there is no reason for the Buddhas to remain in our world because there's not much they can do to lead us on the path. Our merit hooks the Buddhas; it causes teachers to appear. But when we are unreceptive, there is no causal energy to receive spiritual guidance.

The existence of the Dharma depends on our positive potential; it depends on our practice. The presence of teachers, Buddhas, bodhisattvas, and Dharma friends in our life depends on our positive potential. Actually, it depends not just on ours, but everyone's. As one person, we don't usually have enough positive potential to invoke many teachers, so we band together with a group of sentient beings and practice together. Then our accumulated positive potential invokes teachers. This is one of the reasons for having Dharma centers. How often are we going to get one-on-one teachings with a teacher? Not very often. But if we practice with others, our accumulated positive potential makes it possible for teachers to come to our area. Through the force of a number of people sincerely practicing, teachers come to a Dharma center. That's why it is important for people to practice together in groups. I don't have enough merit for His Holiness the Dalai Lama to teach me individually, but the combined merit of 7,000 people is enough causal energy for him to teach.

As a so-called "teacher," I've noticed that teaching in places with centers where people practice together is very different from teaching in places where there is no center, where someone just organized a public teaching and people who don't practice together come. There's a big difference in the kind of teachings that are spontaneously drawn out of me in these two situations.

Some people go to a Dharma center only when a teacher is there. They think, "There's no teacher there so I don't need to practice with the group. Why should I drive all the way to the center? I'll stay at home and practice." Usually when we think like that, we stay at home and don't practice. We may intend to practice, but then the phone rings. Or we think, "Since I have this extra time, I'll do something around the house that I've been putting off doing," or "I'll read a novel that I've always wanted to read." Somehow, we wind up not practicing when we stay at home.

However, when we make the effort to go to the center and practice together with others, some practice definitely gets done. The other people are there for the same purpose, so we don't just hang out wasting time together. We practice, and we feel good about ourselves afterwards. We create virtuous connections with others—that is, collective positive karma. That's why joining together in a group is worthwhile, and why continuing to go to a center whether or not a teacher is there is important.

The example is given of sweeping the floor with one tiny stick or sweeping the floor with a broom. The stick is the positive potential accumulated by practicing alone; the broom is the collective positive potential we generate practicing together in a group. When we come together with others, our concentration is generally better, we don't get up in the middle of a session, and we are more focused. At the end, we dedicate not only our own positive potential, but everyone else's as well. When we engage in group practice, we experience how powerful it is.

This doesn't mean that everyone must practice in a group or that you only practice in a group. People are different, and some find their concentration improves when they're alone. But for most people, the support that a group offers helps them get to the meditation cushion, and once they're there, it helps them to concentrate.

Our practice, on the cushion and in our daily life, creates the causes for the Dharma to exist in the world, for the Buddhas to appear, for spiritual mentors to teach us. If we haven't valued creating positive potential by practicing whatever Dharma we have learned, many of Buddhas will pass into the bliss of nirvana. In other words, their manifestations absorb back into bliss-emptiness.

"Even though they have great compassion" means that from their side, there's connection, there's compassion, there's the wish to help. But from our side there is no connection because we're too busy watching TV, going to the shopping mall, talking with our friends, or watching sports. We have to create the ring with which they can hook us. When we lack the ring of positive potential and genuine interest and aspiration, the enlightened beings enter into nirvana.

"For me there are no other deities, you are my principal deity." This doesn't mean that we don't practice Manjushri, Vajrapani, and Chenresig. It doesn't mean we only practice Tara and forget the other Buddhas. This means that besides the blissful omniscient mind that manifests in the form of Tara, there are no other objects of refuge. In the West, when we are miserable, we take refuge in another "three jewels": in the shopping center, the refrigerator, and the TV. Realizing that these cannot provide the happiness and security we seek, we abandon our refuge in worldly things and take refuge in Tara, who embodies the Three Jewels.

"Bestow realizations upon me, Divine Mother, essence of love." Tara doesn't just bonk us on the head and poof! we have realizations. Rather, realizations come through our practice of learning, contemplating, and meditating on the Lamrim. In addition, when visualizing Tara and reciting her mantra, we imagine all the realizations of the Lamrim flowing into us in the form of green light radiating from Tara. This is how Tara bestows realizations, because when we meditate on her sadhana, our minds and hearts open and are transformed.

"Arouse the great power of your compassion and think of me." As if Tara is not already doing that! Here we're talking to ourselves, saying, "Hey, me! Wake up! Arouse the great power of your own wisdom and think of Tara!" Tara is doing her job already; we have to cultivate and arouse our wisdom and think of Tara.

VERSE 5: DHARMA PROTECTORS

Most Dharma protectors do not show their powers. Tired of those who invoke them, they do not act. Other protectors, lacking insight but proud of their power, may be friendly for a while but will later do me harm. Since I cannot rely on other protectors, you are my principal protector. With divine action, Wisdom Mother, essence of love, arouse the great power of your compassion and think of me.

The first two sentences refer to transcendental protectors, those who are high-level bodhisattvas and Buddhas—for example, Palden Lhamo and Mahakala. Why would they be tired of those who invoke them and not act?

After all, these are great bodhisattvas who manifest in a fierce aspect.

Why are there fierce protectors? Peaceful deities such as Tara have a certain energy that calms and gladdens our mind. But sometimes our mind is so belligerent and stuck that we need the kind of energy that goes "Pow!" to wake us up or to pull us out of unproductive behavior. For this reason, the Buddhas' wisdom and compassion appear in the form of these wrathful deities to demonstrate clean-clear wisdom and compassion that act directly. This active wisdom doesn't vacillate and pamper us. This wisdom doesn't say, "Well, maybe," or, "Poor you. You deserve to be treated well, not like that horrible person treated you." Instead, it's forceful: "Cut it out! Stop those false expectations and preconceptions right now!" Sometimes we need that strong, wise energy to be in our face to wake us up to the fact that our afflictions and old patterns of thought and behavior are making us miserable.

These deities, who are manifestations of this wisdom, are not fierce toward us. They are fierce toward our garbage mind. While they growl at ignorance, anger, attachment, jealousy, pride, and selfishness, they are compassionate toward us sentient beings who are overwhelmed by our disturbing emotions.

Why would a high-level bodhisattva who is a transcendental protector be tired of those who invoke them and not act? Because many times sentient beings invoke them with impure motivation: "Please protect my money. Please protect my possessions. Please protect my status." We request worldly benefit with a self-centered motivation, while the aim of these protectors is to lead us beyond samsara, not just to cater to our petty worldly problems.

Sometimes we invoke protectors and ask for help but don't do our part. A friend told me a joke: Sam goes to the Buddha and prays, "Please Buddha, may I win the lottery," but the Buddha remains silent. Going back the next day, Sam again requests, "Please Buddha, may I win the lottery!" Again, the Buddha is silent. This continues for a week. Finally, after the person requests again, the Buddha says, "Go buy a ticket!"

In other words, we can pray and pray and pray, but if we don't do what needs to be done from our side, what can the Buddhas do? This could be another reason why the Dharma protectors don't act—because from our own side, we don't practice. We stay snug in our eight worldly concerns and don't put in any effort to actualize the path.

"Other protectors, lacking insight but proud of their power, may be friendly for a while but will later do me harm." These are mundane protectors who are not bodhisattvas or Buddhas. They have not entered the path or realized emptiness. When Dharma first went to Tibet, local spirits caused so many obstacles. When they were building Samye, the first monastery, whatever the Tibetans built during the day, the naughty spirits tore down at night. The Tibetans invited Padmasambhava to come to Tibet to subdue these spirits. He did this and made many of them vow to protect the Dharma and Dharma practitioners. He transformed them into worldly protectors. Bound by their vow, they are trustworthy and help His Holiness the Dalai Lama, Tibet, and the Dharma. But other protectors lack insight into Dharma and are proud of their worldly power. We might propitiate them and they may be friendly for a while, but like other powerful ordinary beings their mood may change, and they may later turn against us.

Talking about spirits is normal in Tibetan culture. Their culture is permeated with spirits and protectors. In general, contemporary Western culture isn't, although some people channel spirits and receive messages from beings in other realms. Some of the beings who are channeled may have some Dharma understanding, but most of them are spirits who have some kind of worldly power.

Some spirits have clairvoyant powers that are accurate. Some have powers that are not accurate. Because they haven't entered the path, they lack bodhichitta and the realization of emptiness. Therefore, they are not reliable guides in the way that the Three Jewels are. In Singapore, where I lived for a while, there were temples where people would go into trances and channel spirits who would then give advice and tell fortunes. This is commonly accepted in that society; business people would go to a medium and ask for guidance on their investments and business deals. Sometimes the advice they receive from worldly spirits is good, sometimes it isn't.

In the Tibetan community there has been an ongoing controversy in the last few years because some people have continued doing the practice of a being that they consider to be a transcendental protector. However, His Holiness the Dalai Lama says it is a worldly spirit. Because the practice divides the Tibetan community into factions at a time in history when they need to remain united, he recommends that this practice be abandoned.

In the mid-eighties, many of my friends were getting into protector practices. I never had much affinity for them; I knew that I needed to refine my ethical discipline because whatever happens comes down to karma. But once in a while, part of me doubted: "Am I missing something? Everybody else is doing these practices." His Holiness quelled my doubts. During one spring teaching, he said that Tibetans put too much energy and emphasis on protectors, "You have altars with cabinets underneath them in your homes. You put your valuables in the cabinets and a statue of a protector on top and then ask the protector to guard all your valuables. This is not what Dharma practice is about! You can do protector pujas, beat drums, and ring bells, but if you don't keep your precepts, you create causes for lower rebirths and suffering no matter how many protectors you request to help you. The real protection is taking refuge in the Three Jewels and observing karma." In other words, if we don't take refuge in the Three Jewels and observe karma, even if the Buddha holds our hand when we die, he can't do anything because we haven't created the causes for goodness. Real refuge comes down to our own practice. It's not about asking others to protect our reputation, worldly power, or property. That's why His Holiness has been discouraging people from propitiating spirits.

"Since I cannot rely on other protectors, you are my principal protector." What is Tara? Tara is wisdom that realizes emptiness and bodhichitta, the aspiration for full enlightenment in order to benefit all sentient beings. Tara is the realization of the entire Lamrim, and these realizations are our principal protector. This verse doesn't mean that instead of requesting fierce protectors, we now pray to Tara but leave our bad habits and harmful attitudes as they are. That's not it. Tara's essence is all the realizations of the path. Those realizations are our real protection because when we generate them in our own mindstream, our internal peace becomes invincible. Asking Tara—wisdom and compassion—to protect us means we're committing ourselves to developing these realizations in our own mind.

"With divine action, Wisdom Mother, essence of love, arouse the great power of your compassion and think of me." Again, this is saying, "Me, this person who sits around and procrastinates, may I arouse the great power of my motivation and think of Tara, compassion, and wisdom."

VERSE 6: TRUE NATURE AND ILLUSIONS

To ordinary view the names of objects are the same as their meaning. Like this, they produce afflictions and bind us to samsara. When it is time to die, unless I understand the true nature, could a wish-fulfilling gem enable me to carry even a sesame seed with me? Since I do not trust in illusions, you are my real richness. Please grant my desires, Divine Mother, essence of love. Arouse the great power of your compassion and think of me.

To our ordinary vision, when we say the name of something we think that that name is the same as the object we're referring to. When I say "cup," it seems that this is a cup, doesn't it? It doesn't appear to us that "cup" is a label that is given to an accumulation of atoms arranged in a certain form that is used for the purpose of drinking tea. When we say "cup," cup doesn't appear to us as a label given in dependence upon that base which is performing that particular function. Rather, we think that "cup" is the very essence of this thing. That's grasping at the inherent existence of the cup. We think that the label *is* the thing, that the base *is* the inherent essence of that object.

Similarly, when we say "I," we don't think of "I" as just a label given in dependence upon a body and mind that are constantly in flux. We don't think of "I" as something labeled in dependence upon a body and mind that are interacting in a certain way. Instead, we hold to a fantasy that, besides the body and mind, there's a real "I" there.

We impute the label "I" on the psychophysical aggregates and, not satisfied with that, we think there's something solid within the body and mind that is me, a "me" that exists from its own side independent of other phenomena. Grasping at persons and phenomena as existing in that way is grasping at inherent existence. We think there's a real "I," but the self is only a conventional one, something that exists by being merely labeled by thought. Instead of "I" being just a label that is useful, we think of the self as this real thing that is mixed in with the body and mind.

Thinking there is a real "me," we then want to defend it, protect it, and make it happy. Because we grasp at all phenomena as inherently existent, objects become the cooperative conditions that "produce afflictions and bind us to samsara." There's a real me in there that has to be taken care of, protected, and made happy, so I get attached to the things that seem to make me happy. I get angry with whatever interferes with my happiness. I compare myself to others and am jealous with those who have more, proud toward those who have less, and competitive with those who have the same.

Under the influence of these afflictions, we act, thus creating karmic seeds on our mindstream. These actions, or karma, influence which body we take in our next life, where we are reborn, and what we will experience in life. In other words, our motivations and actions plant karmic seeds in our minds, and when conditions ripen, these seeds bear fruit—our samsara. All of cyclic existence—all the misery, confusion, and torment of sentient beings—comes from this ignorance grasping at inherent existence. It's tragic. We believe, "I'm real and you're real. The things I'm attached to are real. For example, in this baked brown blob, there's a real brownie that's inherently delicious!" But if I chew the brownie and then spit it out, where is that real brownie? If there were a real brownie, it should remain as a real brownie no matter what I do to it. It would be a real brownie even if someone crumbled it up. But it's not.

When we are attached to something, we think that there's a real thing in there with an essence. When we get angry at something or somebody, we think they're real, that they exist from their own side. It appears that there's a real person who is a real jerk, and therefore, our anger is warranted. We don't think, "I'm mad at a label associated with a body and mind." No, I'm mad at *that person* because she's a jerk. The "I" feels very solid, and the other person likewise seems solid. Then we fight a war, each of us trying to protect a real, inherently existent "me" that, in fact, doesn't exist at all.

"When it is time to die, unless I understand the true nature, could a wish-fulfilling gem enable me to take even a sesame seed with me?" People in ancient India believed that wish-fulfilling gems and wish-fulfilling trees existed. If you prayed to a wish-fulfilling gem, it would give you whatever material possessions you wanted. Let's pretend such a gem exists. At the time we die, could that gem give us anything that we could take with us into our future lives? Can any physical object go with us into the next birth? Can our friends and relatives go with us? Can our body accompany us at death? Do our reputation and awards go with us?

What do we take with us when we die? Only the karmic seeds on our mindstream and our mental habits. We develop habits and create karma in the process of trying to procure and protect our possessions, money, reputation, loved ones, and comforts. The karmic seeds from those actions come with us, giving rise to future happiness and suffering, but our vacation home stays here, our partner stays here, our money stays here, our DVDs stay here. All the brownies in the world stay here. We can't take any of that with us. And yet we spend our whole life negotiating in order to fulfill our eight worldly concerns, trying to get the things that please us and avoid the ones that don't. We think that will bring us happiness. Our precious human life, which could be used to progress along the path to enlightenment and to unveil our tremendous Buddha-potential instead is used in the service of the eight worldly concerns.

The big betrayal is that at the time of death, none of those things come with us. We've worked our entire life to get them and then when we die, zip. Even this body that we love and cherish so much, that we try to make so comfortable by feeding it right and exercising it enough, we can't take it with us. We want the right kind of diet so we gain weight if we're too thin or lose weight if we're too fat. If we have straight hair, we curl it. If we have curly hair, we straighten it. If we don't have any hair, we get a special cream to make our hair grow.

The point is: Can any of this help when we die? Whether we have hair or not doesn't matter because our head doesn't come with us when we die. Thinking this is what enabled me to cut my hair in order to ordain. I had long, beautiful hair down to my waist that I had tended for many years while it grew. I thought, "If I die, I can't take it with me anyway, so let's just leave it now."

We can't take our body, our possessions, our friends and relatives, our Valentine cards, love letters, mementos, medals, trophies, or anything of sentimental value with us. None of them come with us when we die. Instead, our relatives have to go through them and throw them away. Think of that. Do you want really want others to look through all the stuff you've saved?

The real jewels are the seven jewels of the aryas:

1. faith, or confidence, in the Three Jewels
2. generosity
3. ethical discipline
4. listening to teachings
5. integrity or self-respect
6. consideration for others
7. wisdom dedicating these virtues to enlightenment

These jewels come with us. They fulfill our virtuous wishes for good rebirth, liberation, and enlightenment and lead us to wonderful results. Faith, confidence, and trust enable our refuge in the Three Jewels to be deep and stable. This is the basis of the rest of our practice. Some people who are new to the Dharma say, "I don't know if I believe in the Three Jewels, but I believe in the value of ethical discipline, generosity, and so forth." Gradually, as they hear more teachings and contemplate their meaning, these people will see that the Three Jewels are nothing other than the embodiment of the excellent qualities that they admire.

Seen in one way, generosity is the completion of the path. In other words, the path is for the sake of developing our qualities and opening ourselves so fully that we don't hold anything back when it comes to being of benefit to sentient beings. Seen in another way, generosity is the first step on the path. It is a quality valued in all religions and among the non-religious as well.

Ethical discipline enables us to be generous without harming anyone in the process. It restrains us from actions that damage ourselves and others. Although various religions may differ on the details of ethical discipline, they all agree that the ten destructive actions create problems in the world.

Listening to teachings allows us to learn the Dharma. It leads to the wisdom arising from listening, which in turn stimulates us to reflect on and meditate on the teachings. Reflection and meditation, in turn, lead to the wisdoms arising from reflection and meditation.

Integrity is a sense of self-respect that inhibits us from acting destructively because we have a sense of our own worthiness. "I'm a Dharma practitioner and value myself as one, so I don't want to talk behind my colleague's back." Consideration for others is restraining ourselves from acting destructively because we value others and know that our harmful actions impinge on their happiness. Others could also lose faith in us and in the Dharma if they see us acting recklessly.

With the wisdom dedicating the above virtues, as well as all others, to full enlightenment, we direct our positive potential so that it will ripen in the form of our highest aims. Unlike external jewels that stay behind when we die, these inner jewels and the positive potential we accumulate from practicing them come with us into our future lives.

"Since I do not trust in illusions, you are my real richness. Please grant my desires, Divine Mother, essence of love. Arouse the great power of your compassion and think of me." Illusions are our thoughts that these objects, people, and situations are of dramatic importance, that they have some inherent essence, that they are the meaning of our life. We think that having money, a comfortable body, a good reputation, and people who love us is the meaning of life. Is that the meaning of life? As human beings, is that all we are capable of actualizing? On one level, those things seem very meaningful. But when we remember that we can't take them with us when we die, that we create a ton of negative karma trying to get them when we're alive, and that we're very seldom satisfied with them even when we have them, then thinking that they are the purpose of our life is an illusion, isn't it?

According to the Buddha, we have incredible human potential that we don't see at the moment, the potential to become a fully enlightened Buddha. Think about it. We have the potential to open our heart and love everybody equally. Isn't that remarkable? Can we even understand that? I think that is pretty outstanding. We have the potential to gain different samadhis so that we can manifest various forms in order to benefit countless beings. Sometimes we hear about the potential that we have and we don't believe it. It sounds too fantastic. "Couldn't be true. I'm just little ol' me. My only potential is to eat, sleep, and go to the bathroom." We look at ourselves with what Lama Yeshe used to call "poor-quality view."

Our mind has Buddha-nature. What incredible potential! When we think about our human potential and see how we are easily and consistently distracted from it, how we waste our time chasing after things and worrying about things that aren't important, we see how our disturbing attitudes and negative emotions cheat us.

Understanding this doesn't mean that we drop everything in our lives and go to Sravasti Abbey. But it means that whatever is in front of our nose at any particular moment is our Dharma practice. Whoever we are with at this moment is symbolic of all sentient beings. We try to cultivate open-hearted love without attachment for whoever is in front of us at that moment. Whether we love them dearly or find them repugnant, we practice overcoming our biased attitudes. Whatever situation we're in, that's our Dharma practice.

Let's stop wasting our time dreaming of a perfect external environment in which we'll practice. The situation we are in and the people we are with right now are the field of our Dharma practice. The present is the only time we have to practice. This attitude is hard to develop. For example, when I'm intent on doing something and someone interrupts me, I have a hard time stopping and paying attention to them because I want to finish what I'm doing. I'm set on doing this and if somebody calls and says, "Hello, can you help me?" I snap at them and return to what I'm doing. In that moment, the person who telephoned is my Dharma practice. But I miss the opportunity to be kind to them because I'm preoccupied with my own agenda. If I saw that person as a representative of all sentient beings and remembered that the purpose of my life is to benefit all sentient beings, I could look them in the eye with kindness and cherish them. I could stop and talk with them with love in my heart.

"I do not trust in illusions." "Illusions" also refers to objects that appear as inherently existent. People and phenomena are like illusions in that they appear one way but exist in another: They appear to exist inherently, independently. In fact, they are dependent through and through.

We say to Tara, "You are my real richness." Tara is the wisdom realizing emptiness so let's not grasp Tara as an inherently existent savior. We have to be careful here. In our ignorance, it's possible to think, "All these worldly things appear inherently existent although they are not. I'll abandon them and instead worship Tara," but meanwhile we grasp at Tara as inherently existent. We must remember that everything—including Tara, the Buddhas, Dharma, Sangha, and our Dharma teachers—are empty of inherent existence. They also exist by being merely labeled. This is the real richness—the wisdom realizing that things exist by being merely labeled and are therefore empty of inherent existence.

With that understanding, we say to Tara, "Please grant my desires, Divine Mother, essence of love." What are our desires? Not Prince Charming or brownies or new skis. Our desire is to gain the realizations of the path so that we can make our life meaningful and benefit ourselves and others. Our real desire is to attain the truth body and form body of a Buddha. Can a wish-fulfilling gem do that? No, only Dharma practice can. We are the ones who make ourselves into Buddhas by practicing what the Buddha taught us. We depend on the guidance of others, but we are the ones who must practice what they teach. We can hire somebody to mow our lawn and do our dishes, but there are some things in life that we have to do ourselves. We can't say, "I'm tired. Can you sleep a few extra hours for me tonight because I don't have any time?" Does that work? "I'm too busy to eat. Can you eat for me so I won't feel hungry?" That doesn't work. Practice is like that; we have to do it ourselves.

Verse 7: Friends

I cannot rely on non-virtuous friends for even a day. They pretend to be close to me and all the while have in mind the opposite. They are friends when they wish it and enemies when they don't. Since I cannot trust in this kind of friend, you are my best friend. Be close to me, Divine Mother, essence of love. Arouse the great power of your compassion and think of me.

Have you ever had a "friend" like this—someone who pretends to be close while they are really trying to get something from you? These false friends are cunning and manipulative. Sometimes they realize they are behaving like this, but at other times they can't see it. Of course, we're never that kind of "friend," are we? We're always nice, honest, and considerate, right? According to our self-centered thought, it's only *other* people that have that fault.

Sometimes we think that if we could only meet the right person or the right group of friends, we'd feel secure and loved. But even people who are very nice can't provide us ultimate refuge, can they? They change, we change, the relationship changes.

Have you ever had a close relationship in which everything went perfectly and you never once felt hurt by something the person said or did? Such a relationship doesn't exist. When we are close and involved with people, our garbage bounces off of each other. We end up hurting each other even though we don't want to. It happens simply because we have uncontrolled minds. That's part of the suffering, the tragedy of samsara. We want to be happy, and we want the people we care about to be happy. But because our minds are filled with afflictions, we hurt each other. We hurt and are hurt by the people we care about.

This is a universal experience. Is there anyone who has never had this experience? It's painful, isn't it? This verse is talking about what happens when we have expectations of limited samsaric beings that they can't fulfill. Our unrealistic expectations bring us a lot of suffering. Sometimes we have false expectations of ourselves, thinking that we should be, do, or have something we don't. Those false expectations likewise cause suffering.

This verse is not implying we should not trust people. We trust people, but we trust wisely. We recognize that people with uncontrolled minds are going to slip up no matter how wonderful they are. And even if they don't slip up from their side, because our mind is all set to misconstrue their words and deeds, we impute harm even when, from their side, they may not have intended any. Each of us has something we're super-sensitive about, and we get all worked up when a dear one pushes this button. Later, when we talk to the person, we learn that they had no intention to harm us. But we were hurt because our preconception factory was working overtime generating lots of presumptions.

Saying, "I cannot trust in this kind of friend, you are my best friend," doesn't mean that we should trust only Tara and not trust sentient beings at all. We can trust sentient beings, but we need to assess how much trust someone can bear and trust him or her to that extent, not more and not less. That may involve revising our level of trust as the other person changes. Recognizing that we're all in cyclic existence, let's try to have reasonable expectations of others and of ourselves. In that way we won't be so surprised when people don't turn out to be what we want them to be.

I don't know about you, but I'm repeatedly surprised when people turn out not to be what I thought they were. Each time it happens, I think, "Wait a minute. I thought you were like this. How come you're not?" Then I have to remember, "Maybe I had some expectations." I make a determination to stop having expectations, but the same thing happens with the next person I meet: "I thought you were like this. How come you're not?"

This verse doesn't imply that we should turn away from sentient beings because we think they're stupid and ridiculous. Rather, we turn away from our preconceptions that create a multitude of problems with other sentient beings. We stop expecting people to be what we want them to be. We stop expecting them to fulfill all of our needs. We stop expecting them to be perfect. Then we can start accepting people for what they are at any particular moment, knowing that they'll change in the next moment. It's a difficult practice, but that's the way to have peaceful relationships.

It can be difficult to accept others and to accept ourselves. "I should be better. I should be something different. I should have more." All of this is conception; it's all mental fabrication. It's just the mind churning up "shoulds," "ought tos," and "supposed tos." All this is conceptual rubbish, and yet we believe it. Part of the solution is to recognize that these thoughts are conceptual rubbish and not reality; this gives us the mental space not to believe them. When we stop believing them, it becomes much easier to accept what we are at any given moment, knowing we will change in the next moment. We'll be able to accept what others are in one moment, knowing that they will be different in the next moment. This is good stuff for everyday practice; it's very practical.

We say to Tara, "You are my best friend." Tara doesn't have a fickle mind.

An enlightened being will be there for us no matter how we treat them. From our side, we usually ignore the enlightened ones unless we have problems. But here we say, "You're my best friend. Be close to me, Divine Mother, essence of love." This helps us to open our eyes and become Tara's friend and be there with Tara. Tara is sitting there with her hand stretched out. This is symbolic—she extends her hand, wanting to teach us and inspire us. But usually we say, "I'm busy today. I've got to take the kids to soccer and finish a project at work." Reciting this verse helps us to change our minds and to see the importance of cultivating a spiritual friendship with Tara.

VERSE 8: REFUGE AND REQUEST

You are my guru, my yidam, my protector, my refuge, my food, my clothes, my possessions, and my friend. Since your divine quality is everything to me, let me spontaneously achieve all that I wish.

This doesn't literally mean that Tara is our clothes, even though it's said that a Buddha can manifest as physical objects. Rather, it means we give up clinging to the eight worldly concerns and clothe ourselves in wisdom and compassion. In other words, practicing Dharma is the meaning of my life; Dharma is the focus of all my energy.

Dharma is true cessations and true paths, the last two Noble Truths. Dharma is the cessations of suffering and the afflictions that cause suffering as well as the spiritual realizations that bring about those cessations. That is everything to us. That's our real refuge, what we can rely on that will never let us down. By relying on the Dharma—by purifying our mind and cultivating all wholesome qualities—may we spontaneously achieve all that we wish.

Tara embodies all objects of refuge—our gurus, meditation deities (*yidams*), and Dharma protectors. Like spiritual food, the wisdom and compassion she represents nourish us. Like clothes, the six far-reaching attitudes she embodies adorn us. Like possessions, the enlightened qualities provide security. Like friends, bodhichitta opens our heart to love and feelings of inter-connection with all sentient beings.

"Let me spontaneously achieve all that I wish." What do bodhisattvas wish for? They desire the enlightenment of themselves and all beings, the flourishing of the Dharma, the ultimate peace of non-abiding nirvana for all beings. I imagine that a bodhisattva could want food, clothing, and possessions, too, but not with attachment for them. These things are useful to stay alive and can be used to benefit others. There's nothing wrong with wishing for them. But attachment that thinks "I've got to have them or I'll be miserable" is a distorted mental state.

The English word "desire" can be confusing, because some translators use it for the same term that I'm translating as "attachment." But the English word "desire" can have multiple meanings, not all of which are negative. For example, we desire to practice the path to enlightenment; we desire the happiness of all beings. We can have virtuous desires; there is no problem with that. Not all desires are attachment. Desires for worldly things that are involved with attachment are to be abandoned on the path, but desires for spiritual goals and benefiting others are to be cultivated.

It's fine to have wholesome wishes and desires. Don't go to the extreme of thinking that avoiding attachment means we don't wish or desire anything, but just sit there like a bump on a log. Such erroneous thinking makes us depressed, "If I don't chase after food, money, clothes, sense pleasures, reputation, and praise, then my life has no meaning and there's nothing to do." Wrong! Our life can be very meaningful. It has great meaning and there's a great deal to do to progress on the path and benefit others. Bodhisattvas have lots of positive desires and aspirations. In fact, arya bodhisattvas are constantly manifesting multiple bodies to benefit beings.

Verse 9: Compassion

Although I am overwhelmed by my habitual, uncontrolled mind, please cut these self-centered thoughts so that I will be able to give my body and my life millions of times without difficulty to each sentient being. Inspire me to be able to develop this kind of compassion to benefit all.

It may seem impossible to aspire to be able to give our own "body and life millions of times without difficulty to each sentient being." When we recall that sentient beings are countless, such an aspiration seems out of sight. But isn't it wonderful to aspire for virtuous things that are out of sight? Doesn't just allowing such noble aspirations in your mind uplift you? Even though it sounds totally impossible, it's wonderful to wish for it anyway.

Someone once said to me, "The aspirations in Mahayana Buddhism, the vows made by the Medicine Buddha and Amitabha, and the dedication to enlighten all sentient beings by yourself alone are too fantastic! How can you aspire for things that are so unrealistic and impractical?" I told him that I love these aspirations because they open me to infinite potential. They create so much space in my mind. I don't expect myself to be able to fulfill these aspirations tomorrow. I don't know if I'll ever be able to fulfill them. But just to have the thought that such a thing could be possible—even to feel that it's possible to have a mental state that wishes for such things—creates joy, enthusiasm, and optimism in my mind. Play with the thought, "Sure, I can give my body and life a million times over and be cool with it! I won't get bummed out, paranoid, or shake in my shoes. I'm okay doing this." See if just letting that idea into your mind makes you feel more spacious.

If we can imagine giving our body millions of times over, then when it comes time to die in this life, we will feel okay about leaving our body. Dying will not seem such a big thing because we've imagined giving our body millions of times for the benefit of sentient beings. If we can recall this visualization at the time of death, it will be easy to feel, "I've imagined giving my body away to benefit beings before, so what's such a big deal about giving this body up when it's time to die? I don't need to cling to this body. I'll let go of this body with the same ease as in meditation, and I'll think I'm doing it to benefit all sentient beings." If we can think about giving up our body during this life, there's a chance this thought will come up at the time of death. If this thought comes at the time of death, dying will be easy. Practicing thinking and visualizing in this way helps our mind.

But let's not become smug thinking that because we visualize altruistically giving up our body that we are actually capable of doing it. I had a rude awakening about this when the second *intifada* began. I'd been going to Israel regularly to teach, but when the suicide bombings became frequent, I postponed one visit, then another. My Israeli friends were upset with me: "We're suffering here. Why can't you come and teach us the Dharma?" I realized that even though every day I recited a verse from *Lama Chöpa* saying, "Even if I remain for an ocean of eons in the Avici hells for the sake of one sentient being, inspire me to complete the far-reaching joyous effort to strive with compassion for supreme enlightenment and not be discouraged," I couldn't even go to Israel for the benefit of a group of interested students. Boy, do I have a long way to go.

I have limitations. I admit it. But it helps me to think, "Maybe someday I won't have those limitations." It gives me hope just to imagine not having them and aspiring to be so compassionate that my mind has no problem benefiting others in whatever way is necessary. For me, just thinking about limitless compassion brings a sense of purpose, meaning, and value in life. If we think like this, then when looking at a sentient being, instead of thinking, "There's Joe Schmoe who's a slob," we will think, "There's Joe Schmoe who has the potential, just like me, to give his body and life a million times over out of true love and compassion for all sentient beings. Wow! Joe Schmoe has that potential! I respect him."

When we can see this potential in ourselves, we can see it in others. Then it's much easier to respect others and to treat them with dignity instead of just brushing them off. If we think that every single person in the Taliban and al-Qaeda has the potential to become a fully enlightened Buddha and manifest millions of emanation bodies for the benefit of all beings, then we can't make them into an inherently existent enemy and hate them. Of course, that doesn't mean we endorse their horrific actions. Instead, we view the situation with compassion: Here are beings who have Buddha-potential but whose minds are so overpowered by wrong views that they think killing others brings happiness. That's a tragedy for them as well as for the people they kill. May they be freed from such incorrect views and use their human potential in a kind and beneficial way in the future. May we help them to do this.

Seeing their situation with a broader view, we'll be able to have compassion for them. We see that what's going on now is a temporary aberration. While we don't let them continue killing and inciting violence, we also don't make them into a solid, permanent enemy and fill ourselves with hatred. If our mind is filled with hatred, our mind has become like theirs. That doesn't help anyone. The Buddha said that hatred is not cured by hatred, but only by love. Meditating on love and compassion enables us to see the tremendous potential in each and every living being; it helps us respect them and see beyond the current karmic bubble that they're manifesting. This gives us a positive and optimistic attitude, and with this, we work for a better future in our world.

"Although I am overwhelmed by my habitual, uncontrolled mind..." This is where we are right now, but it's not where we'll be forever. We accept that at the moment our mind is overwhelmed by habitual uncontrolled thoughts and emotions. But the possibility exists to cut these self-centered thoughts, to go beyond them and cultivate another aspect of ourselves. There is reason for hope and confidence.

This verse articulates our wish to generate bodhichitta, the method side of the path. The next verse expresses our wish to cut the self-grasping ignorance and to actualize the wisdom realizing emptiness, the wisdom side of the path. We often talk in the Mahayana tradition about two great obstacles: one is our self-centeredness and the other is the self-grasping ignorance. These two verses state our wish to overcome both of these obstacles.

VERSE 10: REALIZING EMPTINESS

Empower me to cut the root of samsara, self-grasping, and to understand the pure doctrine, the most difficult middle way, free from the errors of extremes.

The root of samsara—the very cause of our circling round and round in unsatisfactory conditions—is self-grasping ignorance. "Self" in this context means "inherent existence." It doesn't refer to the person or to the psychological ego as conceived by Freud. Our innate self-grasping ignorance grasps at all phenomena, including persons, as having a "self," that is, as having inherent existence. This ignorance holds everything as having its own essence, existing from its own side, from its own accord, under its own power.

As a previous verse said, we confuse the name with the object and think that the name abides in the basis of imputation. We do this in relation to ourselves, other people, and all phenomena. This causes suffering because we make everything concrete instead of seeing things as appearances that exist by being merely labeled.

Instead of seeing things that ebb and flow as dependent on causes and conditions or as dependent on parts, we apprehend them as real, as objectively existing "out there." Furthermore, they appear to have their own essence, independent of the mind that conceives and labels them. This is a false appearance to our senses. Then we mentally hold these false appearances to be accurate; this is grasping at true or inherent existence.

On the basis of grasping our body and mind to be truly existent, we grasp the "I," which in fact is merely labeled in dependence upon them, as truly existent. Then seeing some things around us as inherently existing sources of pleasure, we become attached to them. In our effort to be happy, we try to get more of these "real" things that we think will give this solid "I" happiness. When our desires are frustrated, we become angry and fight against anything that interferes with the happiness of this misconceived "I."

The self-grasping ignorance lies behind other wrong views, too: for example, thinking that everything is fixed, static, and lasts forever; believing that this life is all there is, that past and future lives are non-existent; thinking that the happiness we find in samsara is real happiness and not seeing that it is unsatisfactory in nature because it changes and lets us down; believing that our own and others' bodies are pure, when in fact they're made of disgusting components. Adding these other wrong views to our self-grasping, we become totally confused.

We don't realize just how out of touch with reality our mind is. In the world, we seem normal; we have our individual quirks, but we are basically normal. But when we start looking from a Buddhist point of view at what causes suffering and what causes happiness and how things exist, we notice that our views frequently have nothing to do with reality. For example, we relate to impermanent things as if they were permanent and long lasting. That's why we're jolted when a treasured item breaks or shocked when somebody dies. But think about it: Why are we so surprised? As soon as causes come together to form a new thing, that thing has the potential to disperse, change, and break. Yet when it does, we think, "Wait a minute. That's not supposed to happen." Right there we see how our mind holds false views and grasps something that is transient in nature to be unchangeable. We do this all the time.

All of our wrong views are rooted in self-grasping ignorance. What do we need to do to cut this? First, we need to hear teachings about emptiness, so that we understand exactly what it is that we're trying to realize and what it is that things are empty of. Emptiness doesn't mean emptying our minds of conceptual thoughts and sitting there with a blank mind. If we don't know exactly what phenomena are empty of, we will easily fall to the extremes of nihilism or absolutism. Nihilism is the view that things are totally non-existent or the belief that there's no cause and effect. When we hear teachings on emptiness, we learn that it doesn't mean total non-existence but the lack of a particular type of invalid existence. Things are empty of inherent existence, which has never existed. Correct teachings on emptiness emphasize that although things are empty of inherent existence, they still exist conventionally, dependently.

Absolutism, on the other hand, reifies things so that we grasp at them as having their own independent identity. If we hear correct teachings on emptiness, we won't fall to this extreme either for we'll understand that although things exist on a relative level, they do not inherently exist.

Hearing teachings on emptiness from a qualified teacher and reading texts with the correct understanding of emptiness are very important. In that way, we'll understand what emptiness is, what things are empty of, and how to meditate on emptiness.

Second, we need to think about the teachings and discuss them with others. Asking questions and refining our understanding through contemplation and discussion is essential. Some people hear the word "emptiness," think they know what it means, and devise their own meditation on emptiness. They may meditate on this for a long time, but they won't get anywhere. Or worse yet, they think they have made progress and then teach their wrong view to others. Such ignorance makes more of a mess.

Sometimes we hear teachings and we think we understand, but as soon as we start talking about them with someone, we realize that we don't understand the meaning very well at all. It's actually good when we realize that we don't understand because then we'll learn. We'll inquire and think more deeply. It takes time to understand the correct view and to refine our understanding. It's not an easy process because the words have many different meanings; we can't always be sure that our initial impression is the correct meaning. Thus, discussion is important to clarify the correct view, so that we will gain confidence in it and know how to meditate on it properly.

The third step is meditation, during which we familiarize our mind with the correct view. Some people think they get an initial glimpse into emptiness and that's it, "Now I'm an arya!" Well, not exactly. There are many levels of realization of emptiness, some inferential and conceptual, others direct and non-conceptual. We need to know the stages of the path and to check our meditation experiences with our teacher to make sure we're going in the right direction.

In order to have special insight into emptiness, we have to develop single-pointed concentration. This involves learning the teachings on how to develop concentration and then practicing them continuously.

To develop concentration, living in ethical discipline is necessary. Purification to clear the gross obstacles from our mind—the gross negative karmas—and accumulation of positive potential through practices such as generosity are important. The purpose of the seven-limb prayer and the mandala offering is to purify negativities and accumulate positive potential. For this reason, those in the Tibetan tradition do 100,000 prostrations, 100,000 Vajrasattva mantras, 100,000 mandala offerings, and take refuge 100,000 times. It's not the number 100,000 that's so important; it's the purification and the creation of positive potential that occur while doing these practices. When we do them, we'll experience their effect on our mind. This effect can't be understood intellectually, just as the taste of honey can't be experienced by talking about it.

From our side, we need to hear and learn the teachings, think about them, and meditate on them. From her side, Tara appears as spiritual mentors who teach and encourage us. Tara and her manifestations as mentors in our lives act as role models and give us a kick in the pants when we're lazy. Through this, we will understand the pure view, the middle way that is free from the extremes of nihilism and absolutism. We will gain not mere intellectual knowledge but meditative experience. We won't just experience one glimpse into emptiness, but by our repeated meditation on emptiness, the view will come to permeate our very being. That's how we cut the root of cyclic existence.

Humility, joyous effort, and freedom from expectations are valuable assets on the journey to correct realization. Without them, people might experience what seems to them to be a glimpse of emptiness and then think, "Now, I've got it!" They can become quite arrogant, and that's a big pitfall. Or people have a glimpse and create all sorts of expectations. "That was such a wonderful experience. I understood emptiness. I must be close to enlightenment. I'm almost like Milarepa." But when they go back to their families, they say, "My kids are driving me crazy! Why don't they do what I say?" While their minds still explode with attachment and hostility, they cling to their wonderful meditation experience and try to re-create it. Wanting to repeat that idealized experience, they neglect to see that the anger toward their family is due to the very self-grasping they thought they had eliminated by their wonderful meditation experience.

Sometimes we expect quick results, or we think that one small experience is indicative of a huge change. We're creatures of habit, so we need to slowly develop the correct view and repeatedly familiarize our mind with it. This can't be rushed; it takes time. Just as it takes time and repeated effort to break any habit, the same is true of breaking the habit of grasping at true existence, which has been with us since beginningless time. Rather than get discouraged, let's have accurate expectations and joy in doing the practice.

VERSE 11: BODHICHITTA

Inspire me to practice as a bodhisattva, turning away from what is worldly, dedicating all my virtues to teaching living beings, never for even one instant thinking of just my own happiness. Let me wish to attain Buddhahood for the benefit of all.

In his homage at the beginning of *Madhyamakavatara*, Chandrakirti says that compassion, non-dual wisdom, and bodhichitta are the causes of a bodhisattva:

> The mind of compassion, non-dual understanding,
> And the altruistic mind of enlightenment (bodhichitta)
> Are the causes of the children of the conquerors (bodhisattvas).

For me, these three are expressed in verses 9, 10, and 11 respectively.

In this verse, we generate bodhichitta and aspire to practice as a bodhisattva, turning away from what is worldly. What prevents bodhisattvas from being stained by the world? Their wisdom realizing emptiness ensures the purity of their view and of their motivation. After completing a session of meditative equipoise on emptiness, they do not lose the perspective of emptiness, and thus, they see things as like illusions. Consequently, they can work in the world without being stained by attachment to it, because they know that all these seemingly attractive things have no ultimate essence.

In order to fortify their mental determination to realize emptiness, bodhisattvas first cultivate a strong wish to be free from cyclic existence and attain liberation. As a result, they are not enchanted by the marvelous gadgets, fame, and entertainment that enchant us. In fact, they find worldly things very boring.

For bodhisattvas, the Olympics, ballroom dancing, bowling, or whatever is the newest fad have no appeal. Bodhisattvas may engage in these activities, but these things don't thrill them in the way they thrill us. A sale at the Bon Marché is just not appealing to a bodhisattva. The idea of getting a discount on a flashy new car just doesn't make their day. Upgrading their computer and buying the latest digital camera doesn't jazz them. While bodhisattvas remain involved in the world, they don't get excited about these things. Why? Because they aspire for higher goals, greater happiness, and lasting peace.

A few years back, Bishop Tutu visited Seattle University to receive an honorary degree at a large ceremony. Because I admire his deeds, I went to hear him speak at the ceremony. At the beginning of the ceremony, many professors and deans from the university, the mayor of Seattle, and a representative from the state legislature came to the podium to sing Bishop Tutu's praises. Of course, while Bishop Tutu was working so hard in South Africa years ago, important people didn't back him. But now that he's famous, everyone praises him. While these dignitaries sang his praises, Bishop Tutu just sat there looking totally bored. He was not at all interested. But when he came to the podium and started talking about compassion and equality among people, he came alive and lit up. We're the opposite: when somebody praises us, we're wide-awake. We're not bored at all: "Pour it on. Give me more!"

For genuine spiritual practitioners, praise and reputation aren't appealing. They're like a grade B movie, because these beings have turned away from the world. They don't seek honor and possessions because they realize these things don't bring actual happiness. Instead, they dedicate all their virtue to helping living beings. Their main purpose is to guide, teach, and benefit living beings in whatever way they can.

Bodhisattvas guide us in a variety of ways. Sometimes they do so in formal situations such as a Dharma teaching at a temple or Dharma center. Sometimes they teach by informal contact—through casual conversations or during daily actions. Some bodhisattvas are not recognized as great reincarnates or even as spiritual people, but through their contact with us, they help us create positive karma, teach us, or prevent us from acting destructively. They do not have an agenda, "I am now teaching you this so you better learn it," since such expectations just lead to suffering. Yet, because their entire intention is to benefit, whatever they do becomes of benefit.

I've seen that a lot with my teachers. Several of us long-time students would be with our teacher, ready to eat lunch, go somewhere, or hear a teaching when somebody walks in unexpectedly. Our teacher will spend an hour talking to that person while the rest of us wait. It may be somebody who knows nothing about Dharma. We old students can't get appointments with our teacher because he's so busy, and some newcomer strolls in and our teacher spends an hour with him. Imagine that! The injustice of it all!

After this happened a few times, I began to think, "This is bodhisattva action. However my teacher is able to benefit that particular person, he does, right then and there." It doesn't matter if that person has faith or not, is a Buddhist or not. If there's a way to benefit them, he does. This makes me recall the first conversation I ever had with one of my teachers. I went with someone to meet Lama Zopa Rinpoche's plane at Los Angeles International

Airport, and when he got off the plane, Rinpoche talked to me about dolphins. That was the level of my mind; that was what I could understand at that time. So he spent some time making a connection with this young woman with a short skirt and long hair who thought she was really something by talking to her about what she could understand—dolphins. But somehow, something happened, and I ended up going to the meditation course he taught outside Los Angeles. And that was that. Here I am all these years later.

Don't think that Buddhas and bodhisattvas only manifest to Buddhists, and to Mahayana Buddhists in particular. They seek to benefit everyone! Do you think that a teacher in the Theravada tradition can't be a bodhisattva? Do you think that bodhisattvas can't appear as great Christian saints? Just because someone teaches and appears to practice another religion or another form of Buddhism, does that mean he or she can't be a bodhisattva?

Recognizing certain people as *tulkus*—incarnates of great masters—is a Tibetan cultural event. It isn't Buddhism, although it doesn't contradict Buddha's teachings. The Tibetans invented this system of looking for and recognizing incarnations of great masters. These tulkus received excellent education and guidance when they were young. This system was also a way to pass on property and power in old Tibet. Just because a culture doesn't have a tulku system, it doesn't mean there are no bodhisattvas there. Likewise, just because someone is recognized as an incarnate doesn't mean that he or she is a bodhisattva. That person might have a great deal of positive potential but hasn't yet entered the Mahayana path of accumulation. Or there might be an incorrect identification. Do you think that Tibetan culture is free from politics and corruption?

The way that bodhisattvas and Buddhas work is beyond our comprehension; we can't always tell what's beneficial and what's not. Sometimes it's better if we just let go of our judgments about how we think things are or should be.

Someone once asked, "Since Buddhas appear in so many forms, can it be helpful to regard people who have been very influential in our lives as manifestations of Buddhas and bodhisattvas?" In some situations, it can be. That doesn't mean we see everything that person does as perfect, but we realize that for us, that person is like a Buddha in the sense that he or she has instilled many good values and has prepared us for the path.

After my first meditation course, I went to a donut shop in Los Angeles. On the way back to the car, I saw a drunk sitting in the dirt in the parking lot. Full of pride in my newfound compassion, I gave him a donut. He took it and, without looking up, crumbled it in his hand. The delicious donut that *I* gave him disintegrated and fell to the ground. I have the feeling that this drunk was a bodhisattva teaching me something, appearing in that form to show me something quite important.

"Never for even one instant thinking of just my own happiness." Imagine how much happiness we would have if we never thought about our own happiness for even an instant! The self-centered thought tells us that thinking about our own happiness will make us happy, but in actual fact, thinking about our own happiness makes us overly sensitive. We're easily hurt and offended; we get stuck in self-pity. Thinking about our own happiness under the dictates of self-centeredness makes us more miserable.

Not thinking about our own happiness is a way to actually have happiness. Now, we should not understand this in a co-dependent, dysfunctional way. Some people neglect to pay attention to themselves, but it's not out of bodhichitta and real affection for others. It's due to "supposed tos" or "ought tos," or they're trying to please others out of fear. A lot of ego can be mixed in with neglecting ourselves in an unhealthy way.

Letting go of thinking about our own self-centered happiness is not unhealthy neglect of ourselves. It's done with a wisdom mind realizing that spinning around "me, I, my, mine, and my own happiness" doesn't bring happiness.

We have to be very careful that we don't misapply Buddhist teachings and create weird psychological trips. For example: A friend told me that she had heard so many teachings about the disadvantages of self-centeredness that she started feeling guilty whenever she was self-centered. She thought that guilt was good, that guilt is what you're supposed to feel, because if you dislike your self-centered mind and blame it, then you should feel guilty. She got stuck in berating herself until she realized that guilt does not free us from self-centeredness.

To the contrary, guilt illustrates self-preoccupation. When we feel guilty, the "I" is center stage: "*I'm* so bad." Why feel guilty about being self-centered and amplify the situation? Let's accept that at present we are self-centered. That doesn't mean we're failures or unworthy spiritual aspirants. It doesn't mean we're always going to be self-centered. There is a way to retrain our minds, let go of self-preoccupation, and generate genuine cherishing of others. We're learning that method, we're committed to practicing it; we'll gradually transform our mind and exchange self with others.

"Let me wish to attain Buddhahood for the benefit of all." That sums up everything: The meaning and goal of our life, our motivation day and night is to attain Buddhahood for the benefit of everybody. With that aspiration, our life will be joyful. We'll be optimistic and in touch with our potential. We'll know the potential of all living beings, and our mind will feel energetic and happy. Bodhichitta is the ultimate anti-depressant. It is exactly what we need when we feel confused. Mother Theresa once said:

When I am hungry, give me someone that I can feed,
And when I am thirsty, give me someone who needs a drink.
When I'm cold, give me someone to keep warm,
And when I grieve, give me someone to console.

She didn't say, "When I'm hungry, give me some food. When I'm miserable, send someone who will feel sorry for me and make me feel better." Instead, she advises us to look beyond the narrow confines of our self-preoccupation and cherish others.

VERSE 12: THE VALUE OF VOWS

Empower me to actualize as much as possible the most subtle vows and to keep them without a careless mind, thus becoming the most perfect bodhisattva.

"Most subtle vows" refers specifically to the tantric vows. These are taken on the basis of having received bodhisattva vows, and bodhisattva vows are taken on the basis of having taken refuge and keeping some or all of the five lay precepts or the monastic vows. This is a sequential order. Tantric vows are much more difficult to keep than bodhisattva vows, which are much more difficult to keep than the five lay precepts or monastic vows. So we start at the beginning with abandoning killing, stealing, unwise sexual behavior, lying, and taking intoxicants, and as we become comfortable with these, we gradually add bodhisattva vows and then tantric vows.

In America, many people want to take tantric vows because they are the highest, but they don't want to keep the five precepts. Then misconception mind says, "I want the tantric vows, but don't tell me to stop drinking. In tantra, you can drink." Sure you can drink, but only if your realization of emptiness is such that drinking urine and drinking whisky are equally blissful to you. We have a long way to go!

One misconception in the West is that tantra gives you license to do whatever you want to do. That's not true at all. If we study the tantric vows and tantric practice, that is very clear. In tantra, what one can do at what point of practice is highly regulated. A practitioner is capable of doing different practices at different levels of the path. If one does them without adequate preparation or respect for the vows involved, it may adversely affect their Dharma practice. For this reason, it's essential to understand tantra properly, and for this, we need instructions from wise and qualified spiritual masters. Along this line, I recommend Lama Yeshe's *Introduction to Tantra* and His Holiness's *Deity Yoga* and *Tantra in Tibet*.

If you have already received tantric vows, aspire to keep them purely, without a careless mind. If you haven't, aspire to receive them and keep them purely in the future. Whatever vows we have, we work to keep them with a mind that has conviction in karma, is conscientious, and respects the vows. We don't keep vows with an attitude that sees them as a tax we have to pay to receive the initiation that we want. Rather, let's cultivate the attitude that sees vows as essential for our own spiritual progress, an attitude that wants to practice restraint and therefore wishes to take vows in order to cultivate the mind.

Vows are ways to train and subdue our mind. They help us on the path. The various sets of vows are not external rules imposed upon us by someone else. Instead, vows make us more aware and enable us to subdue our harmful impulses. Because we wish to experience the benefit of living in vows, we voluntarily take them. Nobody forces us to take any vows. It's our choice. We choose to take them because we know they protect us from doing actions that we don't want to do anyway.

Vows are trainings; they are things that we practice. "Without a careless mind" means that we understand this. We respect the vows and are conscientious in observing our behavior and regulating it because we respect our Buddha-potential.

Do we have to be certain that we're up to the task before we take a particular set of vows? It's good to study the vows thoroughly and know what's involved before taking them. We should have some confidence that we'll be able to keep them before we take them; but that doesn't mean that we have to be completely confident that we will keep them perfectly. If we could definitely keep the vows without any transgressions, we wouldn't need to take them. So even though we cannot keep them perfectly, we aspire to train our mind and practice according to them. We might break the vows, and when we do, we can purify them and continue training.

In the case of the bodhisattva vows, if we don't feel ready yet to take the actual bodhisattva vows, we can do the ceremony of aspiring bodhichitta. This is valuable for people to do even if they aren't ready to live in the bodhisattva vows, because generating even fabricated bodhichitta for an instant is worthwhile.

"Thus becoming the most perfect bodhisattva." A bodhisattva is well trained, peaceful, stable, reliable, trustworthy, compassionate, and open-minded. To enter the tantric path, ideally one should be a bodhisattva. At the very least, one should have trained in the bodhisattva path.

VERSE 13: A HUMBLE YOGI

Outwardly, let me be simple in my practice, while inwardly, actualize the depth of the diamond vehicle with a strong wish to practice the two stages. Inspire me to attain enlightenment quickly for the benefit of all.

"Outwardly, let me be simple in my practice." This refers to keeping the pratimoksha vows—the vows of individual liberation. There are various categories of these: the one-day vows, the vows of an upasaka and upasika (male and female lay followers), the vows of a shramanera and shramanerika (male and female novice), the vows of a sikshamana (probationary nun), and the vows of a bhikshu and bhikshuni (male and female fully ordained). These vows are the foundation of the path and are to be cherished. Monastics wear the same clothes: our monastic robes. This cuts through some of our feeling of individualism. We look like other monastics; we have the same hairdo as the others. We give up trying to be physically beautiful so that we can develop our inner beauty.

Being outwardly simple also means being humble. This is the way advocated and practiced by Lama Atisha. Outwardly, there is no big show, no fancy robes, big thrones, or huge entourage. One doesn't make a big deal about oneself: "Look, I'm a great tantric yogi, capable of practicing the completion stage." Truly great practitioners are not ostentatious, but are simple in their behavior and dress. In the *Seven-Point Thought Transformation*, Geshe Chekawa instructs us, "Change your attitude while remaining natural." In other words, internally we transform our mind and practice the bodhisattva and tantric vehicles, but externally we look and act like everyone else.

In recent years, His Holiness has been very pronounced about ostentatious dress and behavior. He speaks unfavorably about those in pre-1959 Tibet who wore fancy costumes and rode ornamented horses. In the West, that would be parallel to wearing expensive brocade and riding in a Mercedes or BMW, that is, making a show as if one were very prestigious. As Westerners, we must avoid encouraging that in our Tibetan teachers. Let them remain simple. In addition, we must remain simple. The fact is that many Westerners like the exotica: big thrones, intricate brocade, long horns, and chanting done in deep voices. In Tibetan Buddhism, there are red hats, yellow hats, and black hats. People compete to get hats; they fight over hats. Such behavior is not Dharma.

Why is there so much emphasis about keeping one's level of practice private, discussing it only with one's spiritual mentor or perhaps a few Dharma friends? The more we talk about our practice—"I've realized this. I've experienced that"—the more we will have obstacles in our practice. Some of those obstacles will come externally; we'll have to keep explaining and justifying our behavior to others. That consumes a lot of time that could be used practicing. Other obstacles will manifest internally: our mind will be tainted with arrogance, and we'll get caught up in defending a self-image we've created.

Geshe Yeshe Tobden and Gen Lamrimpa were Tibetan monks who lived in retreat outside Dharamsala and who taught in the West at various times. They have both passed away since then. They were incredible examples of being outwardly simple but inwardly accomplished practitioners. Gen Lamrimpa didn't like big display. He was very simple and so joyful. He meditated above Dharamsala in a simple hut for many years. I would visit him from time to time when I lived there. His hut had a dirt floor, stone and mud walls, and plastic over the cracked windows to keep the wind out. He would make us tea on an old kerosene stove. He had the reputation for having attained *shamatha*, meditative quiescence, but when asked, he never said anything about it. He never wanted lots of students following him around; he preferred to meditate in seclusion, although he greeted people warmly when they visited.

Geshe Yeshe Tobden meditated in the mountains above Dharamsala for many years. Students at Istituto Lama Tzong Khapa, an Italian Dharma center, where I lived for nearly two years, invited him to come and teach. Many lamas want to go to the West because they live comfortably and receive a lot of offerings, which they give to their monastery. Geshe Yeshe Tobden wasn't interested in any of that. He didn't want to go to the West. He went to Italy only because His Holiness told him to go.

To show respect for Geshe-la as our teacher, we constructed a throne in the meditation hall and housed him in a comfortable villetta. When Geshe-la arrived, we served his first meal on China and gave him silverware. He looked at us and said, "Get rid of this and bring me a plastic bowl." When he went to teach in the meditation hall, he walked right by the big throne with the beautiful cushion we had arranged. He just took a regular cushion, put it on the floor, and sat down. It was an incredible lesson for us. He wasn't interested in being treated as a big lama with pomp and fuss. He didn't care about our admiration; his sole interests were transforming his mind and benefiting others.

When he walked around Dharamsala, Geshe Tobden's *shamtab*—his lower robe—was uneven, and his socks were falling down. He was the kind of monk that people who didn't know him would ignore because he looked raggedy. But he was an incredible practitioner. Even his attendant, Ven. Lobsang Donden, who for years carried food up to Geshe-la's hut every week when he was in retreat, never saw Geshe-la's tantric implements—his vajra, bell, and drum. He never saw any sign of tantric practice, and yet clearly, Geshe-la practiced tantra. He was just a simple and humble practitioner who consistently told us to practice thought transformation. He's a good example for us.

The great Indian sage Shantideva practiced in a similar way. In fact, the other monks used to call him "The One Who Does Three Things." What three? Eat, sleep, and go to the toilet. When we study *Guide to a Bodhisattva's Way of Life*, we can see what an accomplished practitioner he was. But in his life, he was completely humble. Personally speaking, I admire humble practitioners the most. There are many reasons to be humble, and I can't see any reasons to go around declaring oneself to be a realized being.

Having a simple lifestyle and humble appearance accords with the way the Kadam geshes of Tibet practiced centuries ago. It's something for us to emulate, for it will help us to give up the things that we think we "need"—comfort, praise, and reputation.

"Outwardly, let me be simple in my practice, while inwardly, actualize the depth of the diamond vehicle." The diamond vehicle is the Vajrayana. Externally, we are simple, but internally, we practice the profound meditations of the Vajrayana. The bodhisattva practices of the Sutrayana are also profound; we shouldn't think they are easy. For years practices such as equalizing and exchanging self for others and the *tong-len* practice of giving and taking were not taught publicly because they were so profound. Even now, we are instructed to do the taking and giving meditation secretly, without telling others that we are doing it. We shouldn't make a big deal by telling others, "I'm practicing taking and giving. I am taking on all of your suffering. Aren't I compassionate?" The *Eight Verses of Thought Transformation* talk about doing these practices secretly, in a humble way, without declaring to others that one is doing them.

"With a strong wish to practice the two stages." The practice of highest yoga tantra consists of two stages, the generation stage and the completion stage. "Inspire me to attain enlightenment quickly for the benefit of all." By practicing simply on the outside while inwardly intensely practicing the bodhisattva path and the Vajrayana, may we quickly attain enlightenment. We seek enlightenment not because it is fancy and the best but in order to benefit everybody. The reason that fully qualified disciples want to practice tantra is that they want to attain enlightenment quickly because their bodhichitta is so strong. They find other beings' suffering so unbearable that they want to eliminate their own obstacles in order to be of greatest benefit to others as quickly as possible. The best motivation for entering the Vajrayana is this very intense compassion and bodhichitta.

Nowadays, in the West and also in Asia, many people lack that motivation when they approach Vajrayana. They want to receive Vajrayana initiations to get blessings, They seem to think that the less they understand, the more blessing they receive; that the more exotic and incomprehensible a ceremony is, the bigger the blessing. The more bells are rung, the more blessed water they drink, the more rice is thrown, the greater the blessing. This is how spiritually uneducated people think.

In San Jose in 2001, His Holiness taught the *Heart Sutra* for three days and on the fourth day gave a Medicine Buddha initiation. Several thousand more people came for the Medicine Buddha initiation than for the *Heart Sutra* teachings. His Holiness was not happy about that situation. He bluntly said that it should be exactly the opposite, that more people should come for the teachings and fewer should take the initiation. Why? Because everyone needs to practice the three principal aspects of the path—the determination to be free, bodhichitta, and correct view. On the basis of establishing a firm foundation in the Dharma, those who are properly prepared can request and receive tantric initiation for the deities that they wish to practice.

VERSE 14: RELYING ON TARA

Divine Wisdom Mother Tara, you know everything about my life—my ups and downs, my good and bad. Think lovingly of me, my only mother.

That's an amazing thing to feel comfortable saying to someone. Usually, we don't like being so open and vulnerable; we don't want others to know everything about us. We worry that they might criticize or judge us. If we think about the Buddhas' omniscient minds—that they know everything going on with us and still look at us with kindness—then from whom are we trying to hide things? How are we ever going to hide anything from a Buddha?

The bottom line is that each of us wants to be understood, accepted, and loved, don't we? Underneath it all, we don't want to feel that we have to hide our shortcomings or pretend to be something that we're not. Basically, we all want to be accepted even with our faults and imperfections. But how often do we let people accept us? Sometimes, it's hard even to let people love us.

But here, opening up to Tara and accepting that she knows everything about us and still accepts us is psychologically very healthy for us. Tara knows all our ploys, our manipulations, our trips, the ways we hide things from ourselves, the ways we hide things from others, the fronts and images that we create, and she still loves us anyway. It's pretty powerful when you think like that! It's also powerful for us to be totally open: "Think lovingly of me, my only mother." Tara already does this, but saying it reminds us that she does.

Verse 15: Death and Rebirth in a Pure Land

I give myself and all who trust in me to you, Divine Wisdom Mother Tara. Being completely open to you, let us be born in the highest pure land. Set me there quickly with no births in between.

This verse leads us to look ahead and to prepare for our death and rebirth. Most people don't like to think about death. They believe that if they think about it, it will happen, but if they don't think about it, it won't. That's not very logical, is it? Personally speaking, when I first met the Dharma and heard teachers who spoke frankly about death, I was relieved. I had questions about death and what happens after death but until then, I hadn't met anyone who was comfortable talking about it. So I appreciated being able to discuss dying and death—unavoidable experiences that all of us will have—honestly with people who had wisdom.

Why should we aspire to be reborn in a pure land after death? All the conditions there are conducive for practice, so attaining realizations comes more easily. Everything in the environment reminds us of the Dharma, so we will be able to stay focused and are less likely to be distracted from our spiritual aspirations.

Sometimes we pray to be reborn with a precious human life and at other times in a pure land such as Tushita, Sukhavati, or Akanishta. In the "Six-Session Guru Yoga" we aspire to be reborn in Shambhala. You may wonder: Why do we pray for so many different rebirths in these various places? We're covering all our bases!

A precious human life in this world is the best basis for practicing highest yoga tantra, which, in turn, can bring disciples of great faculties to enlightenment in this lifetime. But doing tantric practice properly requires exceptional clarity and strength, and if we are not capable of doing tantric practice or of doing it properly, we could instead be led astray by attachment to the pleasures of this life. Even with a precious human life, we are pulled in a lot of non-Dharma directions, as we know from our own experience. So for some people, being born in a pure land, where the environment is more conducive, is safer.

The beings born in some pure lands, such as Amitabha's Sukhavati, are not necessarily out of samsara, nor have they necessarily realized emptiness when they are born there. But through practicing under Amitabha's guidance, they attain these realizations, become an arya, or noble one, and eventually attain enlightenment. To be reborn in other pure lands, one already needs to be an arya being. Birth in a pure land depends on our view and level of realization. For a highly realized yogi, living on Planet Earth is like being in a pure land. To a person with a pure mind, the surrounding environment appears pure.

It's important not to confuse pure lands with the Christian idea of heaven. Furthermore, a pure land is not nirvana. Nirvana is the state in which we've eliminated all our suffering and the origins of suffering. It is a mental state. We're not born into nirvana. Rather, our mind transforms into the state of nirvana. A person may initially attain nirvana while living in the human realm or in a pure land, but his body doesn't have to go anywhere because it's the mind that attains the state of nirvana.

If you feel more attracted to one pure land, focus your dedications to be reborn there. Also, at the time of death, if there's a pure land that you have a preference for, then pray, "May I be reborn in that pure land or in any other place where I can be of great benefit to sentient beings."

Interestingly, bodhisattvas aspire, "May I be reborn in the hell realms to benefit the sentient beings there." Are we able to pray for that? We may be able to, as long as we're in a comfortable and safe place when we make that prayer. But imagine saying that with conviction when we're dying. Our self-centered thought would have a fit: "If I pray to be born in the hell realms to benefit sentient beings, it might actually happen. Oh no, I don't want that!"

The self-centered mind behind that fear is so evident. It runs deep. By repeatedly doing the series of meditations to develop bodhichitta, we can chip away at that. Don't be discouraged when your mind becomes afraid of suffering. It happens sometimes when doing the taking and giving meditation, too. When it does, we know the meditation is having an effect. Self-centeredness and ignorance are afraid of being eliminated. Instead, we can use that opportunity to recognize the "I" which is the negated object in the emptiness meditation. The inherently existent "I" appears very clearly when we're afraid. Recognize it, and then do the four-point analysis to disprove its existence.

"I give myself and all who trust in me to you, Divine Wisdom Mother Tara." With this powerful thought, we give ourselves to Tara, that is, to wisdom and compassion. This means that we make the development of these and other spiritual qualities of foremost importance in our lives. We give not only ourselves, but also all those who trust in us to Tara, that is, to our highest spiritual aims. At the time of death, clinging to the people we love won't benefit us or them. Separation is definite, and trying to resist the undeniable is futile. So instead of clinging to dear ones, we let go of our attachment and offer them to Tara. Tara's protection, not our possessive clinging, will help them. Wisdom and compassion will lead them to genuine happiness while our grasping at them with attachment and jealousy won't. Entrusting them to Tara, we can die, knowing that our dear ones are in good hands. Needless-to-say, our relationships with them will be better if we relinquish, or at least diminish, our attachment to them now. By not holding on to others as if they were the ultimate cause of our happiness, we'll be able to appreciate and feel closer to them now. Why? Because clinging, possessiveness, and jealousy won't hinder our communication and sharing.

This verse speaks in particular about those who trust us. Those who trust us include our relatives—parents, siblings, and children—and our friends. But it doesn't stop there. Our colleagues, employers, or employees trust us to be honest, responsible, and fair. Disciples trust their spiritual mentors to act with integrity and to lead them on the path. Spiritual mentors trust their disciples to be sincere in their aspirations and to continue practicing.

The world functions based on sentient beings trusting and benefiting each other. Thus, maintaining trust in relationships is extremely important. While we often focus on whether or not those we trust come through for us, we need to expand our perspective to examine whether we are trustworthy to those who count on us. Being worthy of others' trust is an honor, and misusing others' trust inflicts a great deal of pain on them and creates the cause for our own future suffering as well.

What constitutes being trustworthy? One element is taking another's interests and well-being to heart, cherishing them not because we can get something from them but simply because they exist. If we manipulate others for our own selfish benefit, clearly there is no reason for them to trust us. When we use people to satisfy our ego's hunger for pleasure or power, we abuse their trust. For this reason, being mindful of our motivations when relating to others is essential. Should our motivation become crooked due to self-centeredness, one element of mindfulness practice is to recognize this and straighten it.

Verse 16: Kindness Inspiring Practice

May the hook of your compassion and your skillful means transform my mind into Dharma and transform the minds of all beings, whoever they are. They have all been my mother, the mother of one unable to follow the Conqueror's teachings.

Meditating on the meaning of these verses isn't simply praying to Arya Tara as an external being. We're trying to tap into our own Tara-nature, our Tara-potential, so that we can transform our minds into the Dharma. We want to transform not only our own mind but also the minds of all beings—Osama bin Laden's mind, George W. Bush's mind, our boss's mind, the minds of those who are our friends and enemies, and the minds of strangers, animals, and all other living beings. Why? Every person, whoever they are, has been our mother. We have a very close link with each and every sentient being in that they've all been our mothers in many previous lives. One person is our mother of this lifetime, but we've had beginningless mothers in beginningless lifetimes. All beings have been our mothers, and as our mother, they have been kind to us.

Have we stopped to appreciate what our mother did? Who woke up every few hours in the middle of the night for two years to feed us when we were infants? Our parents cared for us when we were helpless infants and couldn't even feed ourselves. Without their care—or the care of whomever they asked to look after us—we would not have survived.

Some people recoil, thinking, "My mother was too busy working to take care of me when I was young," or "My mother was an alcoholic and beat me." But the bottom line is that our mother gave us this body, this precious human life. That alone constitutes tremendous kindness because without this body, we wouldn't have the ability to practice the Dharma. Our parents are limited beings controlled by afflictions and karma, just as we are. They made mistakes, but they did what they could to care for us given their capabilities and their personal situation. Instead of wishing they had done more for us, let's appreciate all they did. Appreciating our own parents is important for being a good parent ourselves.

"One unable to follow the Conqueror's teachings." All these beings have been so kind to us throughout our beginningless lives and have given us so much. Even in this life, we've received so much from other sentient beings. Our ability to practice Dharma depends on the kindness of so many sentient beings. Still, we're unable to follow the Conqueror's teachings in a perfect way. Here we admit our own fallibility. While we aspire to practice the Buddha's teachings, we acknowledge that our practice is incomplete. We are committed to repaying the kindness of others, and the best way to do this is through gaining all the realizations of the path up to Buddhahood. The wisdom, compassion, and skillful means we develop through practice will enable us to benefit sentient beings most effectively. The kindness others have shown us inspires us to practice because from the depths of our heart we feel connected to others and want to help them.

Saying we are unable to follow the Buddha's teachings isn't a statement of low self-esteem. We don't hate ourselves or feel guilty because we haven't practiced the teachings better. Instead, we acknowledge the kindness others have shown us, get in touch with our deep aspiration to become a Buddha, and yet frankly admit our limitations—that sometimes we're lazy, rationalize our harmful actions, neglect our precepts, or are rude. Still, we aspire to do better. We have confidence in ourselves that we can enhance our good qualities and subdue the harmful ones. Aware that we have Buddha-nature, we don't fall into low self-esteem or self-hatred.

In another translation, this phrase appears as: "My mothers, who do not follow the Conqueror's teachings...please transform their minds into the Dharma." With great compassion, wishing all sentient beings to be free from all obscurations and sufferings and to have all joy and bliss, we aspire that they may meet, have faith in, and practice the Dharma. Through this, may the Dharma be totally integrated into their minds, transforming them, so that they attain full enlightenment.

VERSE 17: DEDICATION

By reciting this prayer three times a day and by remembering the Divine Wisdom Mother Tara, may I and all beings who are connected to me reach whatever pure land we wish.

Although Lama Lobsang Tenpey Gyaltsen recommends reciting this prayer three times a day, I don't think that's a hard and fast "rule" or a definite guarantee to be reborn in the pure land. It's not the number of recitations that is important, but their quality. Many verses that we say daily are recited three times because that gives us the opportunity to do it at least once with concentration and sincerity. Training our mind by generating the thoughts and feelings expressed in this prayer creates the causes to be reborn in a pure land. Thus, it is the mental transformation, not the recitations themselves, that leads to rebirth in a pure land.

Here we dedicate the positive potential we've created from this recitation and meditation so that we and all beings connected to us—those to whom we are karmically close, such as teachers, students, relatives, friends—may be reborn in Sukhavati or in whatever pure land we wish. But when we think about this more, aren't we connected with all beings in one way or another? For example, although we don't know the child working at the Nike factory in South America who helped make our shoes, we're connected to him. Although we were born centuries after Catherine the Great and the anonymous serfs in her empire, aren't we connected to all of them in that they influenced the development of Russia, a country with which our country has relations?

VERSE 18: SUBDUING THE FOUR NEGATIVE FORCES

May the Three Jewels and especially the Divine Wisdom Mother, whose essence is compassion, hold me dear until I reach enlightenment. May I quickly conquer the four negative forces.

Asking the Three Jewels and Tara to hold us dear is actually admonishing ourselves to hold *them* dear. They're already holding us dear. We need to regard Tara and the Triple Gem as rare and precious. Through this, we will subdue the four negative forces—the four maras. The first mara is death under the control of ignorance, the afflictions, and karma. Stopping this doesn't mean that we become immortal, but we do overcome painful death under the control of ignorance. The second mara is the afflictions—disturbing attitudes and negative emotions, such as ignorance, anger, attachment, pride, jealousy, laziness, resentment, and so forth. The third mara is the five contaminated aggregates—the five aggregates of body and mind upon which the person, the "I," is labeled: body, feelings, discriminations, volitional factors, and consciousness. The fourth negative force is external beings who obstruct our practice. Another way of describing this fourth mara is our own pride and arrogance that interfere with our practice.

"A Song of Longing" is one of my favorite recitations. Lama Lobsang Tenpey Gyaltsen put into words very profound feelings that resonate within me. We know that he had a close connection with Tara because his words are so potent and bring forth such powerful feelings within us. These verses point the way for us to train our minds. Now, let's put them into practice!

Tara's Ultimate Nature

Tara is the embodiment of the three principal aspects of the path: the determination to be free, the altruistic intention of bodhichitta, and the correct view of reality. When we visualize Tara, we begin with the lotus on which she is seated. The lotus represents the determination to be free from cyclic existence—the cycle of constantly recurring problems and unsatisfactory conditions—and its causes. A lotus grows out of the mud in a pond and becomes a beautiful flower unsullied by the mud. Similarly, we begin in the mud of cyclic existence, and through practicing the Dharma we grow into liberated beings who are untainted by afflictions and contaminated karma.

A flat moon cushion rests upon the lotus. This represents the altruistic intention, the aspiration to become a Buddha in order to best benefit all sentient beings. The radiance of the moon is cooling and calming. Similarly, compassion, which is the root bodhichitta, soothes feelings of alienation and calms anger.

Tara herself symbolizes wisdom, the correct view of reality, that is, that all persons and phenomena are empty of inherent existence. Just as Tara's radiance illumines the world, the wisdom realizing emptiness dispels the darkness of ignorance and illumines our minds. While the determination to be free and the altruistic intention motivate us to seek liberation and enlightenment, it is wisdom that completely eliminates the afflictions and their seeds.

Cyclic Existence and the Correct View

Why is meditation on the correct view important? Because we want to be free from unhappiness, dissatisfaction, and misery. How will meditating on the emptiness of inherent existence bring us peace and happiness? To answer that we have to understand the Four Noble Truths—the unsatisfactory nature of cyclic existence, the factors that keep us bound to it, the state of freedom, and the path to reach it.

Cyclic existence is not something outside of us. It is our body and mind being under the control of afflictions—especially ignorance—and karma. Cyclic existence is repeatedly taking rebirth under the force of afflictions and karma. Propelled by ignorance, we are born again and again without choice. We were born with a body that becomes old, gets sick, and dies, and with a mind that gets upset, spaced out, angry, and filled with desire. Did we choose this? No. We have the illusion that we're in control, but when we look closely, we see that we didn't choose any of these situations.

Since ignorance is the root of the problem, it's important to investigate it, to know what it is, so that we can determine if it can be eliminated, and if so, how. The ignorance that is the root of cyclic existence is not the kind of ignorance that makes someone vote for a foolish political candidate. It is not the ignorance that doesn't know the capitals of all countries. It's the kind of ignorance in which we superimpose a type of existence on persons and phenomena that they do not have. This type of existence is called inherent, or independent, existence. That means that we apprehend things as if they existed out there objectively, with their own essence, with their own inherent unchanging nature, completely independent of our mind and of everything else.

Not only do we grasp external objects and people and our body and mind as existing inherently, but we grasp ourselves as existing in this way as well. When we say, "*I* want this," it feels as if there's a real—that is, an inherently existent—"I" or "me" there. "Don't tell *me* what to do." It feels as if there's an objectively existing "me" that exists by itself, from its own side, under its own power. Similarly, when we look at phenomena, such as a clock, it seems as if there's a real clock there. When we see chocolate, we relate to it as real chocolate existing from its own side. When we're attached to someone, we think there's an objectively existent, real person out there who is inherently wonderful. This is the erroneous view of inherent existence.

Due to the stains of ignorance on our mindstream, everything appears to be real, to have its own separate, independent nature. We assent to this appearance and grasp at everything as if it existed objectively, "out there," inherently. Prominent among all phenomena is this big "I" that's at the center of the universe. Innately, we feel that our life's work is to get everything that makes this self feel good and to destroy everything that makes the self feel bad. All sentient beings who haven't realized the nature of reality have this innate feeling. For example, dogs wag their tails at their friends and bark at their enemies. Similarly, we're nice to the people who help us and mean to the people we don't like. Because we feel that everything has its own nature and that at the center of it all is this solid "me," we think that the way to be happy is to rearrange the external world. This is the view of ignorance. We're so used to seeing things, including ourselves, in this way that we don't notice that it's a view. We never question the way we hold things to exist; we just assume this erroneous view is true.

Under the influence of ignorance, we then overestimate the qualities of someone or something. When we overestimate their good qualities, attachment arises; when we overestimate their negative qualities, anger arises. Motivated by attachment and anger, we engage in many negative actions, or karma. Underlying this process is self-centeredness, which holds that *my* happiness is more important than anyone else's. Thus, we desperately try to get what we want and to get away from or destroy anything that interferes with our happiness. That leads to acting in harmful ways. These negative actions, or karma, leave seeds—traces of energy—in our mindstream. When these seeds meet the proper conditions, they ripen, bringing more unsatisfactory experiences. We react to these new experiences with attachment and hostility, thus creating more karma. This is why it's called "cyclic existence." Under the influence of ignorance, our afflictions motivate actions that create experiences, and those experiences become the setting in which more disturbing attitudes and emotions arise, leading to more actions that create further problematic experiences in which more negative emotions arise. It cycles on and on and on. The root of the cycle is the ignorance that misapprehends how things exist, the ignorance that grasps at true, or inherent, existence.

In this way, it becomes clear that the origin of our unhappiness is not our boss, landlord, ex-husband, or ex-wife. The source of all confusion and unhappiness in our lives is this misapprehension of how phenomena exist and how the self exists.

What, then, is the correct view? It is the wisdom that sees how things actually exist, the wisdom that is free from all fantasized ways of existence. This wisdom knows the lack, or emptiness, of inherent existence. It sees the absence of things existing under their own power, independent of other factors. Since the way ignorance apprehends things and the way wisdom apprehends things are exactly the opposite, they can't both be manifest in the mind at the same time. Just as water extinguishes fire, wisdom extinguishes ignorance. Because ignorance is a misapprehension, an erroneous awareness, it can be counteracted. Thus, when wisdom understands how things actually exist, it overcomes ignorance. If ignorance apprehended things correctly, it couldn't be eliminated. But since it misapprehends how things exist, the wisdom perceiving how phenomena exist can extinguish it. The more we understand the correct view and habituate our minds with it, the more ignorance diminishes until it's totally eradicated and can never again appear in our mind.

When a tree is uprooted, its branches wither and die. Similarly, once ignorance is totally eliminated, anger, attachment, jealousy, arrogance, fear, and anxiety can no longer arise because they are all rooted in ignorance. When these afflictions cease, contaminated actions no longer are created, thus the suffering that they cause ceases forever. That's why understanding emptiness, the correct view, is so important: It's the direct antidote to the very root of all unsatisfactory circumstances. By deepening that view and familiarizing our minds more and more with reality, we purify the mind and become arhats and Buddhas.

INTERPRETABLE AND DEFINITIVE TEACHINGS

The Buddha gave teachings for forty-five years after he attained full enlightenment. Being a skillful teacher, he knew people's dispositions and interests and taught according to their level of understanding. Thus, he did not explain the ultimate nature of reality in the same way to everyone. To skillfully guide them, he taught some people only what they were able to absorb and accept at that time. It was only to fully qualified and mature disciples that he explained the definitive and complete view. For this reason, not all sutras describe the ultimate nature of phenomena in exactly the same way.

After the Buddha passed away, loose groups formed, based on particular sutras and their presentations of the ultimate nature, or selflessness. Later commentators, using reasoning and analysis, identified certain presentations of selflessness as interpretable and others as definitive. Interpretable explanations or sutras give a provisional description of emptiness that requires further interpretation in order to reach the final view, the Buddha's actual intent or meaning. Others are definitive—that is, the view of emptiness they present is the final or deepest one.

What Doesn't Exist: The Negated Object

The Tibetans categorized holders of various Buddhist philosophical views in India into four schools of tenets. One of the distinguishing differences between them is the negated object, sometimes translated as the "object to be refuted" or the "object to be negated." This is the object we believe in that doesn't, in fact, exist. The negated object is what the correct view sees as non-existent.

There are different levels of subtlety of negated objects, and it's interesting to examine our mind to see how each one appears in our minds. The grossest negated object is an unchanging (permanent), unitary (partless), and autonomous (independent) self. This is the self, person, or "I" that is similar to the Christian idea of soul or the Hindu idea of *atman*—an essence that is really us. The first quality, permanent or unchanging, means it doesn't cease or change in any way. Do you have the feeling that there is some soul inside you that doesn't change at all, a soul that is who you are? We may think this essence or soul doesn't change, but simply goes somewhere else when we die. That is, we are the same person if we're in a male body one life and a female body the next.

The second quality, unitary or partless, means this soul doesn't have parts. It's indivisible. It's one solid package. The third quality, autonomous, means that it's independent of our body and mind. It is also independent of causes and conditions. The soul is not influenced by other factors.

Many of us were brought up with this idea of a soul, or a real self. The view of a true soul may be very comforting to some people. Someone who is afraid of death may comfort himself by thinking, "There's something that's me that doesn't die. I am just transported out of this body and will go to heaven." Although the person may find this view soothing, according to the Buddha such an unchanging soul doesn't exist. For this reason, it is called a negated object, and the concept that grasps it is called a misconception. This isn't our only false conception of the self, but it is the grossest. If we search to find such an unchanging, unitary, autonomous self, we can't find it.

People believe in some things that don't exist. The belief in the existence of a soul or an unchanging self exists. That belief exists, but a soul or self doesn't exist. Thus, there are two things: (1) the negated object, which doesn't exist, and (2) the conception grasping at that negated object, which does exist.

A bit more subtle than an unchanging, unitary, autonomous self is the next level of negated object, the self-sufficient, substantially existent self or person. Two different analogies are used to describe it. Both deal with the relationship between the self, person, or "I," on the one hand, and the aggregates—the body and mind—on the other. Let's examine if we hold ourselves to exist in either of these ways. In the first analogy, the self resembles a shepherd and the aggregates resemble sheep. The "I" is the shepherd that takes charge and bosses the aggregates around, which, like sheep, follow along. The "I" takes charge and guides the body and mind. Just as the sheep depend on the shepherd, who is a separate agent, to move, the body and mind depend on the "I," which is something separate from them, to control them. Do we have that feeling about ourselves? Do we feel that there is a real "I" somewhere that is the boss or leader in charge of the body and mind?

Another analogy regarding the relationship between the aggregates and the self is that the aggregates are like salespeople and the self is like the head salesperson. The salespeople depend on the head salesperson. The head salesperson is their leader, but isn't totally separate from them. He, too, is a salesperson. Similarly, the "I" is chief and is the boss of the aggregates, but it's not completely different from the body and mind. Here the feeling is that the mental consciousness—the consciousness that thinks and mentally perceives—resembles a head salesperson. The mental consciousness is the "I" that bosses the aggregates around. The mental consciousness is itself an aggregate, but it's still the head of the aggregates. It exists among them but is more important.

In European philosophy there was the idea of a homunculus—a little person in our pituitary gland that was the "I" or person. The homunculus was in the body but was also the boss of the body and mind. This reminds me of the scene from *The Wizard of Oz* in which the wizard puts on a fiery display, a big ego trip, until Toto, the little dog, pulls back the curtain and exposes the person pulling all the switches. The feeling of the self-sufficient substantially existent self is that there is an important person who is running the show, someone who pulls the switches and makes the body and mind act. We have a feeling that there is a real "me" that is in control; that there's a little homunculus in there controlling the body and mind. There's a wizard behind the curtain pulling the levers, making it all happen. This is the second level of misconception.

A further level of misconception is grasping at an inherently existent self, sometimes called a truly existent self. This is the ignorance that is the root of cyclic existence according to the Prasangika tenet system, the Middle Way Consequence school, which is said to be the most accurate philosophical view. The negated object, an inherently existent self, appears to be mixed with the body and mind but also has its own nature. It doesn't appear as separate from the body and mind, but it doesn't appear to be one with the body or mind either. It is somehow independent but also it's mixed in. We feel that there is an "I" in here, a self or real person somewhere in this body. It's not separate from the body and mind; but it's not totally unified with the body or mind either.

There is the feeling of a real "me," as in "Don't tell *me* what to do!" and a real "my," as in "*My* reputation is at stake!" How does the "I" that doesn't want to be told what to do appear to exist? It seems to exist under its own power. It's really there. It doesn't depend on anything. "Don't boss *me* around!" That "I" doesn't appear to depend on the body or the mind. It doesn't appear to depend on causes and conditions, or on parts, or on the mind that conceives it, or on the label that the mind gives it. That "me" is there under its own power; it is the lord ruler of the universe. So don't tell the ruler of the universe what to do! We feel, "How dumb others are! They try to tell *me* what to do. Don't they know better? *I* know what's best. Everyone should do things *my* way." Such a strong feeling of "I" is the ignorance grasping at an inherently existent "I." The "I" that is grasped at is the negated object.

Another example of how the "I" appears is the feeling, "Poor *me*!" We're very good at feeling sorry for ourselves: "Poor me. Nobody loves me. Nobody appreciates me. I'm always left out. They don't invite me. Everybody else gets the good things. I'm the inferior one. They don't respect me. Poor me." Do you ever have this feeling of "poor me"? How does the self, the "I," appear to exist at that time? It appears to be quite solid. It feels as if there is a solid person that is definitely worthy of the pity of the entire universe. "Poor me. I'm so stupid. I can't do anything right. My brother and sister always get more attention than me. They're more successful, and I'm a failure." The way that the "I" appears to exist when we feel "poor me" is the negated object.

When we're sunk into the mental state of "poor me," we feel the "I" exists as it appears, as a real "me" that inherently and indisputably is to be pitied. We don't think of that "I" as being a hallucination created by ignorance.

Similarly, if someone tried to point out to us that we should question the existence of the "me" in "Don't tell *me* what to do!" we'd tell him that we exist and he should stop telling us what to do! We not only misconceive how the "I" exists, but we also think that misconception is accurate. We don't even realize the level of ignorance and misapprehension we have. That's why problems and confusion abound in our lives. We have no idea how much ignorance pervades our mind.

SEARCHING FOR THE NEGATED OBJECT

Let's search for the person who is "poor me." If such an inherently existent person in fact exists, we should be able to find him or her. Can we identify who or what we are and draw a line around that, saying, "This is me"? Who is "poor me"? Where can we find "poor me"? If we cut our body open, does "poor me" come out? Who is this "poor me" that we so whole-heartedly believe exists? We live our lives as if there's somebody solid and real who is "poor me," but who do we find when we search?

Is there some part of our body that is "poor me"? Neither the skin, muscles, bones, nor organs is "me." Is the brain "me"? If there is a brain on the table in front of us, is a person there?

Let's examine our mind. Is there some part or aspect of our mind that's "me"? We can't identify one of the sense consciousnesses—visual, auditory, olfactory, gustatory, or tactile—or the mental consciousness as who I am. None of our emotions or thoughts is who we are. They are simply passing mental events.

Is the "I" separate from our body and mind? If so, we could locate a person totally separate from that person's body and mind. But that is not possible. Who is the "me" who doesn't want to be told what to do? The next time someone tells us what to do and we feel so strongly that an independent "I" exists, let's try to find it. We have a strong feeling that there is a real "I" but when we search for it, it's difficult to pinpoint anything as being "me."

Buddhist texts describe a number of different methods to search for an inherently existent "I." Chandrakirti explained one using a cart as an example of the "I" and the relationship between the cart and its parts as an example of the relationship between the "I" and its components, the body and mind. Using the example of an external object helps us to search for inherently existent objects, for we not only grasp at our self as truly existent but at everything around us as truly existent. We relate to chocolate, cars, other people, careers, possessions, our body and mind, all as if they were inherently existent, as if there were something there that was really them.

Living in the seventh century, Chandrakirti used the example of a cart because that was an object to which people were attached. One's cart was important for one's livelihood. These days we can substitute a car. What's the relationship between the car and its parts? To identify a car that is findable upon analysis, we'll have to find it either among its parts or separate from its parts. There's no third place it could be. There are seven ways by means of which we can examine the relationship between the car and the parts of the car:

1. Is the car inherently one with its parts?
2. Is the car inherently separate, or different, from its parts?
3. Does the car inherently possess its parts?
4. Does the car inherently depend upon its parts?
5. Do the parts inherently depend upon the car?
6. Is the car the collection of the parts?
7. Is the car the arrangement of the parts?

If the car inherently exists, it should be found in one of these seven ways.

1. Is the car inherently one with its parts?
Think of that BMW you've dreamed of owning. If it were inherently one and the same as its parts, since there is one car, there should be only one part. But the BMW has more than one part. Or if there were many parts to a BMW, then there would also be many BMWs. That doesn't work either. If the car and its parts were inherently the same, there should be either one part since there is one car or many cars since there are many parts. Neither of these is possible. If we look through all the parts—the engine, axle, tires, spark plugs, hood, seat, and so forth—can we identify one of them as the car? The steering wheel is not the car. Would you say "Look at my BMW" and point to a steering wheel on the ground? No. Thus, the car is not inherently one and the same as its parts.

2. Is the car inherently separate, or different, from its parts?
If the car were inherently different from its parts, the car and the parts would have absolutely no relationship; they would be totally distinct and unrelated. Are the parts and the car totally unrelated? Can the car break down without one or more of its parts breaking? Can the car go somewhere without its

parts coming along? The car and its parts are linked; they are related. If the car is sold, so are its parts. If they were inherently separate and unrelated, we could sell all the parts without selling the car or we could sell the car without selling the parts that comprise it. Neither of these is possible.

The car and its parts are neither inherently one nor inherently separate. How does that seem to you? Do you think, "Wait a minute. I know there's a real car there. It's somewhere inside but separate from its parts. We just haven't found it yet." If that thought arises, your analysis is working. It's challenging your deeply held belief.

3. Does the car inherently possess its parts?
There are two ways of possessing something: (1) possessing it the way we possess a dog, that is, the two things are separate and unrelated; or (2) possessing it the way we possess our ear, that is, the two things are related.

Does the car possess its parts in either of those ways? If the car possessed its parts the way we possess a dog, then the parts and the car would be separate and unrelated. We determined in point 2 above that the car and its parts are not inherently separate. If the car possessed the parts the way we possess our ear, then they would be related. Are they inherently related? Are they inherently one? No, we determined in point 1 above that they're not exactly the same thing. So the car does not inherently possess its parts. Conventionally, we can say, "The car has parts," but here we're searching for inherent, not conventional, possession.

4. Does the car inherently depend upon its parts?
5. Are the parts inherently dependent upon the car?
These two points examine the dependent relationship of the car and its parts. The car is the thing that is dependent, and the parts are the basis upon which the car depends. The car is the labeled object and its parts are the basis of labeling. Sometimes the dependent thing is called the "supported" and the basis is called the "support," in which case the car is the supported and the parts are the support. Is this relationship between "support" and "supported" an inherent one?

In a case of inherent dependence, the above two questions could be reworded: Does the car exist inherently in its parts? Do the parts exist inherently in the car? These questions are founded upon seeing the car and its parts as inherently different and separate.

Sometimes when we think of that object parked on the street, it seems that the parts are prominent, that the parts came first and the car came afterwards. First we notice the parts, and then we pay attention to the car that appears to be in them. An analogy of this type of relationship is a lion and a jungle. The jungle is prominent, and in it a lion struts around. The parts are analogous to the jungle and the car to the lion. The car exists somewhere in those parts, roaming around in the parts. The parts are more extensive and the car is there inside them.

At other times, it seems that the car is prominent and the parts are not as important. First we notice the car, and then we fill it in by realizing all the parts are there. We may change the tire, but an inherently existent car is still there. One analogy for this relationship between the car and its parts is yogurt in a bowl. The car resembles the bowl, and the parts resemble the yogurt contained in it. First there is the bowl, then we put yogurt in it and the yogurt takes the shape of the bowl. Another analogy is a forest and snow: The forest is the parts, but the snow covers all the parts. It spreads over the parts and is more extensive than they are. Sometimes we feel that way about the car: "Car-ness" covers all the parts.

We may never have examined our ways of looking at things in such depth before. Try to be aware of this as you perceive various objects throughout the day. Check up if you see the relationship between an object and its parts in different ways at different times.

If the car were inherently dependent upon its parts or the parts inherently dependent upon the car, the car and its parts would be two unrelated objects like a jungle and a lion, a bowl and yogurt, or a forest in snow. However, in point 2 we refuted the possibility of the car and its parts being totally independent of each other.

The car and the parts depend on one another because one can't exist without the other. We can't have a car without having the parts of the car, and we can't have the parts of the car without having the car. Someone might say, "This is a spare tire that isn't attached to a car but it's still a car part, so the parts come first and then there's the car." This is true if we're talking on the conventional level. Since we already know the names and concepts "car" and "car parts," we look at a tire and call it a "car part." But before cars were ever made, if a tire were there, we wouldn't call it a "car part" because we would have no notion of a car. Only when various things come together do we say "car" and "car parts." We can't have one without the other. The car and its parts are dependently related. The car and its parts depend on each other, but they don't inherently depend on each other. If they are dependently related, they cannot be inherently related because the two are opposite.

6. Is the car the collection of the parts?
We might say, "The collection of the parts is the car." It seems that after we put all the parts together, we have the car, so the collection itself is the car. If it were, we could collect all the parts in a heap—the axle, tires, engine, hood, pistons, distributor, transmission, seats, glove compartment—and there would be a car. Can you drive a heap of parts at a junkyard? The collection of all the parts may exist, but if the parts aren't assembled in a certain fashion, there isn't a car. Instead, there's a mess. So the collection of the parts is not the car.

7. Is the car the shape of the parts?
If we arrange the tires, pistons, and so forth in a certain shape, is that shape a car? The shape of each individual part is not a car. When we put these parts together, each one does not take on a new shape, so we still cannot say that the shape of the parts is a car. Furthermore, if the shape were the car, we should be able to drive the shape, but that's impossible.

We've examined seven different ways that an inherently existent car could relate to its inherently existent parts. Can we find a truly existent car that exists in any of those ways? When we analyze, we can't find an inherently existent car in relationship to its parts no matter how we look at it. We can't find a real car in or among its parts, and we can't find a real car totally separate from its parts.

What, then, is the relationship between the car and its parts?

THINGS EXIST BUT NOT INHERENTLY

Since we cannot find a car after searching for it with ultimate analysis, does that mean the car does not exist? No. The car exists, but not inherently. We get in the car and drive somewhere every day, so the car must exist. Neither the car nor its parts exist inherently, but both exist conventionally. The car is merely labeled in dependence upon its parts. We can't find a car in the parts, and we can't find the car separate from the parts. The car exists by being merely labeled in dependence upon its parts.

When we say "merely labeled," it means there's nothing findable there when we analyze and search for a real thing that is it. It means that aside from the label that is given to these parts, we can't find something that is a car. There's not an inherently existent car there, but there isn't no car either. Can you sense that when we say "car," "car" is a label that is given in dependence upon the arrangement of these parts in a certain way so that can perform the function of carrying people and things somewhere? The car exists by being merely labeled in dependence on the parts. It's not one of the parts; it's not one with all the parts; it's also not totally separate from the parts. There's no independently existent car to be found when we search with ultimate analysis, but there is a conventionally existent car that we can use to drive somewhere.

If we could find a car that existed from its own side without depending on anything, we would be able to isolate some discrete object and say, "This is the car." That would mean that an ultimately existent car would be there, because that car could be found when we analyzed and looked for something that was it. However, we just investigated in seven ways and couldn't find anything that existed in that way. But when we don't analyze and just accept things as they appear to us, we can say, "Let's get in the car and go to the Dharma center." There is a car to drive and it takes us there. That car is the conventionally, or nominally, existent car. It exists as a label given in dependence upon other things that are arranged in a certain way. So the car is nothing more than what's labeled in dependence on these parts. There's no real car there, but there is a car there. We drive the car, but we can't find the car when we search for its ultimate existence.

Thus, it is said that the car is empty of ultimate or inherent existence, but it exists conventionally. How does it exist conventionally? It exists dependently by depending on its parts and upon the mind conceiving and labeling "car." The car exists dependently and does not exist independently or inherently. We give the name "car," but the object labeled "car" is not a real car from its own side independent from our mind and the label given it. The problem is that we forget that we labeled "car," and instead think there's a truly existent car that exists from the side of the parts. Then we get attached to it. We don't become attached to a car that's a mere label because there's nothing inherently there to get attached to. Thus, realizing the ultimate nature, emptiness, liberates the mind from attachment, anger, jealousy, pride, confusion, and all other afflictions.

What Carries the Karmic Seeds?

In the same way that there is not an inherently existent car, there is not an inherently existent person that can be found when analytically sought. Go back to the seven points and substitute "I" for car, and body and mind for parts. What is the relationship between the person and his or her body and mind? On the one hand, if we were inherently one and the same as our body, we couldn't say, "I'm thinking," because the body doesn't think. If we were inherently one and the same as our mind, we couldn't say, "I'm walking," because our mind can't walk. Are we the collection of the body and mind? If neither the body nor the mind is inherently "me," how could the two of them together become a person who is findable under analysis? For example, if an apple isn't a pen and a carrot isn't a pen, how could the collection of these two non-pens become an inherently existent pen?

On the other hand, if we were inherently different from our body and mind, the "I" and the body and mind would be totally unrelated. In that case, our body and mind could be on one side of the room and we could be on the other. In sum, however much we search trying to find an inherently existent person that is a real, truly existent "me," we are unable to identify anything. This is the meaning of saying, "The 'I' is empty of inherent existence."

Does that mean that we don't exist? Clearly not; I wrote these words and you are reading them. Both of us exist. However, we don't exist as a solid soul or Self that is the "essence of me." Instead, we exist dependently. The "I" exists by being merely labeled in dependence upon the body and mind.

We may wonder: If there is no findable essence that is "me," what carries the karmic seeds from one life to the next? If there's no inherently existent person that "carries" them, then couldn't one person create the karmic cause and another experience its effect?

All Buddhists and non-Buddhists who believe in karma and its result are challenged to explain how karmic seeds go from one life to another. In general, most non-Buddhists assert some kind of soul, *atman*, or unchanging self that they say carries the truly existent karmic seeds. How do Buddhists, who assert selflessness, explain this process?

This has been an important topic of discussion among the various Buddhist tenet schools. Some assert that the collection of mental and physical aggregates is the person or that their continuum is the person. They say there is a factor called "acquisition" that prevents the loss of karmic potencies as this person goes from life to life. Others say a subtle form of mental consciousness is the person and it carries the karmic seeds. Whereas our body dies, the mental consciousness continues on to the next life and takes the karmic seeds with it.

Other Buddhists assert another consciousness, in addition to the five sense consciousnesses and the mental consciousness. It is a storehouse consciousness, called "mind-basis-of-all," "foundational consciousness," or in Sanskrit, *alayavijnana*. As the repository for the karmic seeds, it travels from one life to the next. This foundational consciousness is said to be the person, the "I," and because it continues from one life to the next, it allows for the connection between the person who created the karma and the person who experiences the result.

Because the Prasangika school refutes inherent existence, it says that there is no fixed, inherently existent thing that is the carrier of karmic seeds. Instead, it asserts that the "mere self" carries the karma. We may wonder: The mere "I" exists by being merely labeled, so how can it carry the karmic seeds? According to the Prasangikas, there is no self that can be found other than the mere "I" that is designated by the mind in dependence upon its basis of designation, the aggregates. That mere "I" is what carries the karma. Furthermore, karmic seeds exist by being merely labeled. Inherently existent karmic seeds also cannot be found when sought by means of ultimate analysis.

But don't think that because there are no truly existent karmic seeds that we don't have to purify our harmful actions. In the same way that although there's no inherently existent car, we can still drive a car, there are also no inherently existent karmic seeds, but karmic seeds still produce results. Although happiness and suffering do not exist inherently and cannot be found under analysis, they do exist, and happiness is preferable to suffering.

According to the Prasangikas, the basis in dependence upon which we label "I" is constantly changing. We have many different consciousnesses—grosser levels of consciousness, subtle levels of consciousness, sense consciousnesses, mental consciousness. Whatever is prominent at a particular moment becomes the basis in dependence upon which we impute "I," although it is not the "I." No fixed or permanent person is there.

For example, when we say "Seattle," our mind that grasps at true existence thinks of a fixed thing. To us, Seattle appears to be one solid unchanging thing. But what we label "Seattle" changes from day to day. The buildings change from one day to the next. Today a building is standing; a week later the bulldozers have torn it down. The people in the city change each day; someone is here one day and moves away the next. So the basis in dependence upon which we label "Seattle"—the buildings and inhabitants—is changeable. We can't isolate or delineate a fixed Seattle or a fixed collection of things that is labeled "Seattle." Nevertheless, we still say, "I'm going to Seattle," and people understand what we mean. Likewise, although there is no inherently existent "I" in the aggregates, when we say, "I'm walking," others understand our meaning.

If there is no findable "I" or person, how do Tibetans recognize the incarnations, or tulkus, of previous great masters? Understanding this is important, because in my observation, it seems that grasping at inherent existence influences the way in which some people relate to the tulku of their teacher. They seem to think the child is the exact same person as their teacher and expect him to have the same personality. But while the child exists in the continuum of what was their teacher, he is not exactly the same person. The aggregates—the body and mind—are different. Because the basis of designation has changed, the person labeled in dependence upon it has also changed. A great master does not have a fixed mindstream or soul that goes from life to life. Rather since his or her aggregates are constantly changing, an inherently existent person cannot be found, and the mere person exists by being merely labeled.

Because the "I" is empty of inherent existence, having genuine self-esteem is possible. If we meditate properly on emptiness, as our understanding of it deepens, our self-esteem will increase. It's the grasping at inherent existence that produces low self-esteem because our self-hatred, guilt, and fears are founded upon grasping at a truly existent "I." The object our low self-esteem holds is an inherently existent "I." Through analytical meditation, we discover that there is no fixed, inherently unlovable, disgusting person. Such a person cannot be found. He or she does not exist. Seeing this, we will no longer be weighed down by hating someone who doesn't exist. A tremendous feeling of freedom comes from realizing that there is no solid person here who is shameful and unworthy. Seeing this, our hearts will be light and joyful. The more we see the "I" as empty, the more we understand that we can become Buddhas and the more we progress on the path to Buddhahood.

While emptiness itself is not difficult—as the ultimate nature of all phenomena, it's present here and now—understanding it can be. If emptiness were easy to perceive, we would have directly realized it a long time ago and would no longer be confused. Patience and perseverance are essential in studying, thinking, and meditating on emptiness. One day we will succeed in eliminating all defilements from our mind and becoming Buddhas. This is the same path that Tara cultivated in her mind. If we follow her example and practice with diligence and compassion just as she did, we will attain the same enlightened result.

10

Emptiness and Dependent Arising

TARA, EMPTINESS, AND DEPENDENT ARISING

WHAT DOES understanding emptiness and dependent arising have to do with Tara? Tara is the embodiment of the wisdom that understands emptiness, dependent arising, and the fact that they are complementary, not contradictory. That wisdom, which does not have color or shape, manifests in the form of Tara in order to communicate with us sentient beings. Thus, Tara is an enlightened being, a Buddha.

In addition, Tara herself is empty of inherent existence. We cannot find an inherently existent Tara when we search for her with ultimate analysis. Nevertheless, Tara exists dependently. She is merely labeled in dependence upon an enlightened mind and the green light body that it manifests. When meditating, we contemplate, "Tara is empty but appears. She appears but is empty." This helps us to understand the complementary nature of both ultimate truth—emptiness—and conventional truth—dependently arising appearances.

EVERYTHING IS EMPTY

Due to subtle obscurations on our mindstream, everything appears inherently existent to us ordinary beings. In addition, we assent to this appearance and actively grasp at things as existing inherently. "Grasping at inherent existence" is also translated as "conception of inherent existence." For me, the term "grasping at inherent existence" has more feeling to it. I get the sense of how tightly I'm holding on to my view.

Although everything—ourselves, our friends, our body and mind, our house, job, reputation, and so forth—appears to exist inherently and we grasp everything as existing inherently, when we search for an ultimate or inherent nature, using the reasoning analyzing the ultimate, we can't find one. For example, while conventionally we can search a room to find the book we want to read, if we search for the room's inherent existence, we won't find it. All we find is its emptiness of inherent existence.

When we search for an inherently existent person who has compassion—the "I" or agent of the compassion—we can't find a person who has compassion. When we search for inherently existent sentient beings for whom we have compassion, we can't find them either. A sentient being is not the body, the mind, the collection of body and mind, or something separate from the body and mind. We can't isolate something, such as the person's body or mind, and say, "That is the real, truly existent sentient being for whom I have compassion." Sentient beings are empty of inherent existence.

Furthermore, if an inherently existent sentient being existed, that person would have to be permanent. Why? Because inherent existence means independent existence, and if something is independent, it doesn't depend on causes and conditions to come into being. Something that does not arise due to causes and conditions and is not influenced by them is permanent. However, every sentient being, as well as his or her body and mind, is changing moment by moment. Whoever we have compassion for is transient. In the very next moment that person has ceased, and a new person in that continuum has arisen.

What is this compassion that we're cultivating? Can we identify and isolate one single thing that is inherently compassion? Which moment of mind is truly existent compassion? Whatever moment of mind we isolate and say "This is real compassion" is gone the next moment. If it were truly existent, it would have to be permanent and unchanging, but each moment of compassion ceases in the very next instant. Is the thought wishing sentient beings to be free from suffering inherently compassion? Or is compassion merely labeled in dependence upon that thought?

What is the enlightenment that we seek to attain through cultivating compassion? Is it three clouds up and turn left? Where is enlightenment? Does enlightenment exist inherently? When we search and try to find enlightenment with ultimate analysis, we can't find something that really and truly is it. Try to find some inherently existent negative karma to purify or some inherently existent positive potential to dedicate. Whenever we use an analytic mind to search for something's ultimate, final nature, its deeper mode of existence, what we find is its emptiness of inherent existence. We can't find an inherently existent thing. All that analysis realizes is that thing's lack of independent existence. That analytic wisdom finds only emptiness. The object that we're analyzing can't bear ultimate analysis, and so the apprehension of an inherently existent object disintegrates.

THE TWO EXTREMES

Someone might say, "If we can't find suffering when we analyze, then why try to be free from it? And if there's no real compassion, what is there to cultivate? Why should we expend all this effort if none of these things exist?" This person has fallen to the extreme of nihilism; he has confused the absence of inherent existence with non-existence. He thinks that because things don't ultimately exist, they don't exist at all. But suffering, happiness, and compassion do exist. They exist conventionally. On the conventional level, suffering hurts and compassion brings comfort. Therefore, eliminating one and cultivating the other has purpose. We know that from our own experience.

The Middle Way view is difficult to find. When we don't find real compassion when we search for it with ultimate analysis, we tend to think there's nothing at all. This is the extreme of nihilism. In fact, we're negating only inherently existent compassion, not conventionally existent compassion. Compassion exists, but not ultimately. It exists only conventionally. On the other hand, as soon as things appear to our mind when we're not using ultimate analysis in meditation, we grasp them as having an inherent nature. This is the extreme of absolutism.

We seem to vacillate back and forth between the extremes of nihilism and absolutism, thinking that nothing exists and thinking that everything has a "solid" nature. Initially, these two views seem to be exact opposites because one holds that nothing exists and the other holds that everything exists inherently. But actually, their premises are very similar. Both views are based on believing these two premises:

1. If it exists, it inherently exists, that is, inherent existence and existence are the same, and
2. If it doesn't inherently exist, it is totally non-existent, that is that the emptiness of inherent existence is the same as non-existence.

Based on these erroneous premises, nihilists and absolutists come to two different conclusions. Those holding the absolutist view say that since everything exists, it must inherently exist. Otherwise, if it were empty of inherent existence, it would be totally non-existent and that can't be. Those adhering to nihilistic views say everything lacks inherent existence; therefore, nothing exists at all.

Neither of these views gets at the truth, because they are based on the same misconceptions. Both views confuse existence with inherent existence and emptiness with total non-existence. Both nihilists and absolutists think existence and inherent existence are synonymous. Both believe emptiness and total non-existence are synonymous.

When teaching the Middle Way view, the Buddha explained that existence and inherently existent are different and that emptiness and non-existence are, likewise, not the same. According to the Middle Way view, emptiness and dependent arising come to the same point: that is, because things exist, they are empty, and because things are empty, they exist. How do they exist? Dependently, conventionally, nominally, in relation to other things is the way in which all phenomena exist. They are dependent on other factors—on causes and conditions, on parts, on being conceived and labeled by mind. Only the Prasangika Madhyamaka, the Middle Way Consequence school, is able to see emptiness and dependent arising as non-contradictory. If something exists, it can't inherently exist. It must be empty. Why? Because nothing inherently exists. Why? Because when we search for inherent existence we can't find it.

Dependent Arising and Emptiness

Although we may not have put our own view in so many words, we may also share the above two premises. Things appear to us as if they had their own real, findable essence and identity, and we innately assent to this appearance and apprehend things to be truly existent. But do they actually exist in that way? With analytic wisdom we must investigate how they exist in order to determine whether things exist in the way they appear to us.

We may think that something exists, but only when we search for it can we say for sure whether it exists or not. Let's make an analogy using everyday, conventional analysis. (Conventional analysis investigates something in the conventional world, while ultimate analysis examines its deeper mode of existence.) For example, we may think we have $100 in our wallet. But when we look in our wallet, there are only a few coins. Believing $100 was there doesn't mean that it was. Similarly, we believe that things have their own ultimate nature and exist by their own findable essence; we instinctively feel that everything has something inside of it that makes it "it." For example, we assume that there is something inside of me that makes me "me," always me, inherently me. We relate to external objects in a similar way: We feel that there is something in this clock that makes it a clock. It's not a microphone. It's not a grapefruit. Why not? Because there is "clockness" nature in it. That's the way it appears to us, and we assent to that appearance. We grasp it as existing in the way it appears.

But does it exist in the way it appears? If something existed inherently, it would have to be permanent and unchanging. Something that has its own inherent nature would exist from its own side without depending on causes and conditions, parts, or concept and label. It would also not depend on relationship with other objects but would exist independent of everything else. Something that exists independently isn't produced by causes, and it can't have effects. If it's not produced by causes, it is permanent and unchanging, because only causes have the power to change something.

For this reason, Prasangikas say that if something arises dependent on other factors, it must be empty of inherent existence. If it existed independently, it would be permanent. But all these things, including "me," are not permanent. They are transient, produced by causes and conditions. Because something is produced, it has a dependent nature. Therefore, it doesn't have its own inherent nature. It doesn't set itself up or exist under its own power because it depends on its causes to exist. It depends on its parts to exist. It depends on label and concept.

Someone might ask, "Are permanent phenomena, such as unobstructed space and emptiness itself, also dependent, or do they exist inherently?" They, too, are dependent. While they do not depend on causes and conditions because they are permanent phenomena, they do depend on parts, concept and label, and other phenomena. For example, the table and the table's emptiness of true existence depend on each other. The table's emptiness can't exist if the table doesn't exist. Furthermore, just as the table exists by being merely labeled by mind, so does emptiness itself. Emptiness does not have its own absolute, independent entity.

Thus, all phenomena—impermanent and permanent ones alike—do not exist inherently, from their own side. For this reason, the Prasangikas say that if something exists, it must be empty. In his *Treatise on the Middle Way*, Nagarjuna said:

> In that (system) in which emptiness is suitable, all is suitable;
> In that (system) in which emptiness is not suitable, all is not suitable.

In other words, because things are empty, it's suitable to affirm their existence. Someone who asserts that things are not empty of inherent existence has difficulty establishing that they exist and function. In a world where things are empty, cause and effect work. Since the system of cause and effect works, things change. Because change is possible, we can become Buddhas. If there were no cause and effect, if we had our own inherent nature, if we had an unchanging, autonomous soul, then we could never become Buddhas. Furthermore, a baby could never grow up, because that person would inherently be a baby. We could never learn anything because learning involves change.

We may say that things change, but inside we feel that at the core there's a solid, unchanging "me." Then, around the edges of this real, unchanging "me" some change can occur. In other words, we feel, "I am the same person as yesterday, just a little bit about me may have changed."

Is this feeling realistic? Can something be totally permanent and independent while a little part of it changes? Is there anything about us that does not change moment by moment? Biologists tell us that every cell in our body undergoes constant change, and physicists say that the subatomic parts that compose our body are in continuous motion. When we learn something or grow older, we change. When we meditate, we see how quickly our thoughts, emotions, and sensations change. If all the things of which we are composed change, there can't be something solid and independent that's a real "me." If there were something solid that is truly and indisputably me, I couldn't change.

Since each moment of body and mind is gone in the next moment and a new moment of body and mind arise, how can the self that's dependent on them be permanent? It can't—unless we say that the body and mind change and there's a permanent self or soul that is separate from the body and mind. But what could an unchanging soul or self do that the body and mind can't do? If we say, "I'm separate from the body and mind. I'm inherently different than and totally unrelated to my body and mind," then what does this "I" do? What is its function?

We may say, "I think," but actually it's the mind that thinks. We may say, "I feel happiness and pain," but it's the mental factor of feeling that experiences these. We may say, "I walk," but we don't need an independent "I" to walk because the body walks. We may say, "I make decisions." Here, too, an "I" that is unrelated to the aggregates isn't possible, because the mind makes decisions. What does this "I" do that neither the body nor mind can do? Can a person who is completely unrelated to the body and mind exist?

If there is a separate "I" that is unrelated to body and mind, we should be able to isolate it and identify it clearly. This means that it must do or be something that's totally separate from body and mind. We may say, "My soul— 'I'—goes from life to life." But examine: Are we the same person as in our previous life? Are we exactly the same person as the baby our parents held? When we examine closely, we begin to see that since things function, since they arise in dependence on other factors, they can't be permanent. They can't exist inherently.

As we investigate, we come to see that many of our thoughts view things in a way opposite to the way they exist. These aren't thoughts we learned in school but are innate misconceptions that we've had since beginningless time. Based on these innate misconceptions, some people may develop a philosophy that justifies them. Thus, we may think there's a permanent soul or that the body and mind are like puppets and the "I" is the puppeteer that controls them. But when we try to find these things with analytical reasoning, we come up empty-handed.

Since things exist, they must be empty. We know from our experience that things do exist. If nothing exists, then what is the book you are reading? There's a person reading a book, a book that's being read, and the act of reading. These things and activities exist. However, they do not exist in the way that they appear. They appear to exist with their own inherent nature, whereas they do not. Therefore, they are empty.

It goes the other way, too. Since things are empty—since we can't find anything when we search for it with analytical wisdom—therefore, things exist. At first that may sound strange. But just because we can't find this pen with reasoning analyzing the ultimate doesn't mean the pen doesn't exist at all. That's the mistake made by nihilists. They say, "Reasoning analyzing the ultimate is the ultimate wisdom, so if something exists, that wisdom should realize it. However, since reasoning analyzing the ultimate can't find things when it searches for them, nothing at all exists."

In actual fact, just because we can't find something with ultimate wisdom doesn't mean it is non-existent. That ultimate wisdom only sees the ultimate nature of things. It doesn't see the appearance level of things. Conventional existence is not in the purview of that ultimate wisdom. So just because ultimate wisdom doesn't find this pen, it doesn't mean the pen does not exist. It means the pen is empty of inherent existence because that ultimate wisdom was searching for an inherently existent pen. It was not searching for a conventionally existent pen.

For example, just because our visual consciousness doesn't perceive the sound of the bell, that doesn't mean the sound doesn't exist. Why? Because the visual consciousness only sees colors and shapes, sounds are beyond its purview. The sound of the bell is established by the auditory consciousness.

Similarly, reasoning analyzing the ultimate can't perceive conventional objects; it searches only for ultimately existent ones. Since it can't find these, we can say that ultimately existent objects don't exist. However, conventionally existent ones still can. They are established by our ordinary six consciousnesses—our five sense consciousnesses and our mental consciousness.

The point is that things are empty, not of existence but of inherent existence. Because they're empty of inherent existence, they exist. How do they exist? They exist dependently. They exist as appearances. They exist conventionally. But they don't exist inherently.

Uniting Dependent Arising and Emptiness

As mentioned before, the views of Buddhist sages in ancient India have been classified into four major philosophical schools of tenets. The first three schools are often called the "lower schools." They assert that because the pen, for example, is a dependent arising—because it exists dependently—it inherently exists. The Prasangika Madhyamaka—the "highest," that is, the most accurate school—says that because the pen exists dependently, it is empty of inherent existence. The lower schools and the Prasangikas both say the pen is dependent, but they draw opposite conclusions from this. The lower schools say that if it exists, it must inherently exist. If it's a dependent arising, it must inherently exist.

The people who adhere to these views are sophisticated thinkers. Why do they assert that phenomena exist inherently? They mistakenly think that emptiness of inherent existence means that nothing exists. If nothing exists, then the law of actions (karma) and their results would not exist. In that case, the ethical basis of life would be undermined and people would think, "Since everything is empty and there is no law of karma and its results, let's do whatever we like because our actions won't bring results." Clearly, such a belief would create chaos in society. In addition, individuals with such a belief would create innumerable causes for miserable rebirths due to their negative actions. To avoid the wrong view thinking that their actions don't bring results, the lower schools assert that because things arise dependently, they exist inherently, and therefore, the system of cause and effect functions.

Prasangikas assert the opposite; they say that because things exist dependently, they are empty of inherent existence. Examine closely: How can something that arises dependent on other factors exist inherently? Dependent existence and inherent existence are contradictory. Inherent existence means it is independent of other factors. How can something be independent of other factors and arise dependently at the same time? It can't.

However, things can be empty and dependent at the same time. Think about it. If something had a fixed, unchanging nature, it couldn't arise due to causes and conditions. It would be able to set itself up by its own power. For example, suppose there were a real me sitting here—permanent, unchanging, commander of body and mind, in charge of the show, a real controller who can't be influenced by anything because of being totally independent. Sometimes we feel, "*I'm* in control. *I* make my own decisions. *I* exist under my own power. *I'm* the boss."

If there were such a fixed and solid "I," it couldn't make any decisions, because making a decision involves change. To make a decision we have to think. When different thoughts occur one after another, our mind changes and we change. There can't be an immutable controller that's totally separate and removed from everything else. It's impossible. An inherently existent controller can't control anything, because to control something involves change.

Because there isn't a fixed, inherent me, I can change. A baby can become an adult; a human being can become a Buddha; rebirth happens; actions bring results; a seed grows into a sprout. All these things are possible because they're empty of an inherent nature, of an independent essence that makes them "them." Therefore, because things are empty, they exist and function. Because they are empty of inherent existence, they arise dependently.

The Challenge

The most difficult and challenging part of this process is to identify the negated object—that is, inherent existence. We have to identify the inherently existent "I" or inherently existent object that we grasp as real. We are so used to holding on to things as inherently existent that we can't even recognize that we're doing it. We take for granted the appearance of inherent existence; we consider it normal. That's how things exist to us. We don't question that appearance, but readily assent to it as true.

Imagine someone being born with sunglasses but not knowing it. Everything she saw would be shaded, and since this would be the only thing she ever saw, she would naturally think that this appearance of shaded phenomena were true. She would firmly believe that things really were that color. Why would she doubt what appeared to her senses? Things have always looked that way. If someone were to say that things weren't really shaded, she would say, "What are you talking about? This tree must exist in the way it appears to me. If it didn't, there wouldn't be any tree here at all."

From the viewpoint of those of us who haven't been born with sunglasses, she is confused. She believes the false appearance to be true. Also, she is unable to separate the shaded quality from the tree. For her, the two things are mixed. If she thinks there's no shaded quality, she believes there is no tree there at all. This is similar to us. We're so used to seeing everything as inherently existent that we don't even recognize what the appearance of inherent existence is. We can't identify what it is we're grasping. If someone says that things don't inherently exist, we think they're negating all existence whatsoever.

Many years ago, I studied *Madhyamakavatara* with Geshe Sonam Rinchen in India. When he would explain emptiness, we students would often look at him and say, "Geshe-la, this doesn't make any sense!" He would respond, "That's because you don't understand the negated object." As I've thought about his words over the years, I've come to see that when I'm confused about emptiness, it's usually because I haven't properly identified the negated object.

The challenge is to identify the negated object. What would inherent existence be like if it existed? Try to identify the grasping at inherent existence when it arises strongly in your mind and then look at the object it apprehends. The masters advise us to recall an extreme emotion to help us identify the inherently existent "I." For example, recall a time when you felt, "Don't tell *me* what to do. Don't boss *me* around," or "*I'm* not wrong," or "Don't accuse *me* of doing that!" Usually when such an emotion arises, we're completely involved in it and caught up in thoughts of how to retaliate or how to prove we're right or innocent. But now let's stop and observe how this "me" appears to exist. Don't describe it in words to yourself, but get a sense of what this "me" is. There is a strong feeling of a real, solid "I." We don't question the existence of that inherently existent "I," we assume it exists because it feels so real.

When I was living at a monastery in France, we nuns would go to Nalanda Monastery where the monks lived for our classes with Geshe Tegchok. One day one of the monks, who was a good friend of mine, said, "All the nuns have to leave within a half hour of the end of the teachings." Immediately I thought, "You're prejudiced against *me*. You can't tell *me* I have to leave!" I was furious. After the teachings, I said to my Dharma brother, "We've got to talk about this." These monks were not going to tell us nuns what to do! So we took a walk, and after both of us let go of our anger, we got it all worked out. Then he looked at me and said, "I think we just missed an excellent opportunity to notice the negated object." We had forgotten to observe the way the "I" appeared to exist when we were upset, and once we were calm again, the negated object was no longer so obvious.

Another good time to identify the negated object is when we're very attached to something. "I really want a relationship. I need money. I need to be loved. I want to be acknowledged for all the good things I've done." Such a strong feeling of a solid "I" often arises during the content of our internal dialog. Sit down some time and write down all the things that you think you need. Do a little inventory of everything you want or need. Notice how there's so much emotion around the possibility of getting or not getting it. "No one loves me! I need somebody to love me!" At that time we're so wrapped up in needing and craving, that we don't observe how the "I" that needs all these things appears to exist. Now, while the neediness is manifest, with one corner of your mind, observe how the "I" appears to exist.

Observing the negated object is a delicate process. If we observe the feeling of "I" too intensely, it fades away. If we don't observe it at all, the emotion overwhelms us and the opportunity is missed. Practice is required to keep the strength of the feeling of "me," and at the same time observe how the "I" appears to exist.

Observe inside yourself: What's the feeling of "I" when I'm upset, and what's the feeling of "I" when I simply say, "I'm walking." What is the difference between the way the "I" appears in those two instances? When we just say "I'm walking," the feeling of "I" isn't very strong. But when we have the strong feeling, "*I* want to be loved!" the way the "I" appears is different.

Investigating our own mind and experience is very important. It's relatively easy to say a lot of words about emptiness: "Emptiness is the lack of inherent existence. One directly perceives it on the path of seeing. There are sixteen divisions of emptiness, but there are also eighteen and twenty divisions, depending on how they are counted. The first one is…"

Intellectualizing about emptiness is not too difficult. It requires study, but it doesn't necessitate experience or meditation. However, study alone won't lead us to liberation. It is crucial to look inside ourselves and examine how our mind works. We won't know the difference between "I'm walking" and "*I'm* walking" unless we observe our own mind and investigate how it holds the "I" to exist. Let's examine: How do things appear to my mind? How am I holding them to exist? Do the things I apprehend exist in the way they appear? This is what Dharma practice is about. We apply the teachings by doing the research in our own mindstream. That's why His Holiness the Dalai Lama says the real laboratory is inside of us.

PRACTICAL APPLICATIONS

Lama Zopa Rinpoche teaches a way of doing walking meditation that incorporates meditation on emptiness. Walk slowly in a peaceful place. As you walk mindfully and calmly with your body and mind relaxed, contemplate: What am I doing? I'm walking. Why do I say, "I'm walking"? Think about it for a minute.

Then slowly ponder: I say, "I'm walking" simply because the body is walking. There's no other reason to say, "I'm walking," except for the fact that the body is walking. Therefore, the "I" is dependent on the body. Without the body walking, I couldn't say, "I'm walking." Because the body is walking, I label, "I'm walking." Thus the "I" is dependent on the body. The "I" is merely labeled in dependence upon this body and mind. There's no "I" other than the "I" that is merely labeled in dependence upon the aggregates.

Although we label, "I'm walking," because the body is walking, we are not our body. If the person were the body, then a dead body could walk.

Because a mind is connected to that body, we give the name "I" and say a person is walking. In the case of "I'm walking," the "I" or person, is labeled in dependence upon a mind being present even though the body is the prominent basis of the label "I" at that time.

When you go to the shopping mall, instead of becoming entranced by the beautiful things that your craving desires, observe: I say, "I'm shopping." Who is shopping? Who or what is the "I" that is shopping? Focus on that for a while.

Then investigate: What is the action of shopping? What is the action of shopping that the "I" is doing? Is the action of shopping the body walking past the stores? Is it going into the stores? Is it looking at the articles for sale? Is it giving the salesperson some colored plastic or paper so that we can take the object home? What is shopping? We feel like shopping is a real thing. We do it all the time. But what really is this action of shopping?

When we search for a real action of shopping, we can't find one isolated thing or event and say, "This and only this is shopping." Instead, many things are going on, and we can't find one of them that is shopping. What we finally have to conclude is that the action of shopping exists by being merely labeled in dependence on there being stores and a body that is connected with a mindstream walking past the stores. That mind is curious about what is in the stores, and the mental factor of attachment is about to arise or has already arisen. People inside the stores are willing to exchange pieces of green paper for the objects in the stores. On the basis of this series of events, we say, "I'm shopping."

Then investigate: What is being shopped for? I say, "I'm shopping for shoes," but what are shoes? Are they the soles? The sides? The laces? The heels? There is nothing to isolate that is really a shoe. Rather, "shoe" is labeled in dependence upon a combination of parts arranged in a certain way.

We see that since there is the action of shopping, there also has to be an agent who is performing that action as well as an object of shopping, the shoes. These three are dependent upon each other. One cannot exist without the other two. However, we don't always feel that way. Sometimes it seems to us that first the agent, the shopper, "me," exists, and then the shopping and the goods come. At other times it seems that first the desirable objects, the goods, are there, and later the shopper comes along and finally the shopping occurs. But in fact, a person does not become a shopper without goods and shopping. Goods don't become the object of shopping without a shopper and the action of shopping. Shopping doesn't become an activity unless there is someone doing it and something being purchased. The agent, the action, and the object are dependent on each other. They don't exist independently, in their own right. They become what they are only in relation to the other two and because our minds give those things certain labels. If we investigate in this way when we're in a shopping center, we'll save a lot of money because there won't be much opportunity for the mind to generate craving!

When we observe and ponder in this way, we notice a difference between how we ordinarily perceive things when we're not mindful of emptiness and dependent arising and how they appear to us when we focus on their interdependence. What's the difference? Inherent existence. That's also the difference between "I'm walking" and "*I'm* walking," and between "I'm hungry" and "*I'm* hungry."

If sentient beings are empty, whom do we love? When we look at a dear one and say, "I love you," who is it that we love? We may point to someone: "Him. That's who I love." Who? What is he? His body? Which part of his body? His little toe? His brain? We sometimes think the brain in the essence of a person. If that were the case, we would say, "I love you, dear," when looking at our loved one's brain.

Or we may think, "I love his mind." The mind has many parts. There are sense consciousnesses, the mental consciousness, and mental factors. Which mind do we love? The mind that is sleeping? The angry mind? The mind that agrees with my ideas? The mind that motivates his mouth to utter sounds that my mind labels "pleasing" while his eyes look toward me with a glance that my mind labels "affectionate"?

Who is it that we really love when we say "I love you"? Can we find some inherently existent person out there that we love? When we search for a real person with a definite, fixed, inherent personality, we can't find him. There's nobody there. Does that mean that there's no person at all? No. We love the person who exists conventionally, the person who exists by being merely labeled in dependence upon a body and a mind. That body exists by being merely labeled in dependence on arms, legs, intestines, liver, blood, spleen, and lymph. That mind exists by being merely labeled in dependence on many different types of consciousnesses—visual, auditory, mental, and so forth—and mental factors—various attitudes and emotions. Even though all these things are merely labeled in dependence on their bases, they still exist. They exist dependently. They are empty of independent existence.

Although no inherently existent person can be found, we still love a person. In the same way, although there are no inherently existent sentient beings, we can still have compassion for them. Our compassion doesn't inherently exist either. What is compassion? Compassion is a moment of consciousness that wishes sentient beings to be free from suffering. In dependence on many moments of mind that have a similar quality of wishing sentient beings to be free from suffering, we label "compassion." Compassion exists by being merely labeled. It's not some concrete thing we have to force ourselves to feel. The sentient beings for whom we have compassion exist by being merely labeled. Because the agent (the one who feels compassion), the action (the compassion that is felt), and the object (sentient beings) exist by being merely labeled— because they exist dependent on each other—therefore, they're empty. They can't be found under ultimate analysis.

In meditation, we keep going back and forth like this—analyzing to search for the inherently existent thing that we're grasping and, not finding it, seeing that it's not totally non-existent because something that exists by being merely labeled is there. Sometimes we start by contemplating dependent arising, thinking of the causes and conditions, the parts, and the mind that conceives and labels—all the factors that are necessary for something to exist. Doing so, we understand that the object is empty of inherent existence. We come to understand that because it's empty, it exists dependently or conventionally, and because it's a dependent arising, it's empty of inherent existence. Dependent arising and emptiness come to the same point, they complement each other; they are not contradictory. Contemplating dependent arising causes us to understand emptiness, and contemplating emptiness causes us to understand dependent arising. At this point, we have the correct view that is free from the two extremes of absolutism and nihilism. As Je Tsongkhapa said in *The Three Principal Aspects of the Path*:

One who sees the infallible cause and effect of all phenomena in cyclic existence and beyond and destroys all false perceptions of their inherent existence has entered the path that pleases the Buddha.

Appearances are infallible dependent arisings; emptiness is free of assertions of inherent existence or non-existence. As long as these two understandings are seen as separate, one has not yet realized the intent of the Buddha.

When these two realizations are simultaneous and concurrent, from the mere sight of infallible dependent arising comes definite knowledge that completely destroys all modes of mental grasping. At that time, the analysis of the profound view is complete.

In addition, appearances clear away the extreme of inherent existence; emptiness clears away the extreme of non-existence. When you understand the arising of cause and effect from the viewpoint of emptiness, you are not captivated by either extreme view.

The concluding verse of that text reads:

In this way, when you have realized the exact points of the three principal aspects of the path, by depending on solitude, generate the power of joyous effort and quickly accomplish the final goal, my spiritual child![8]

Here Je Rinpoche encourages us to practice. After we have gained the correct understanding of the unity of emptiness and dependent arising by hearing and contemplating the teachings, we should deeply meditate in a solitary place that is free from distractions. In this way, we will be able to cleanse our mindstreams completely from all defilements and develop our good qualities to their fullest extent. Then, just as Princess Yeshe Dawa did, we, too, will become Tara.

8. Translator unknown.

Glossary

AFFLICTIONS Attitudes and emotions such as ignorance, attachment, anger, pride, jealousy, and confusion that disturb our mental peace and propel us to act in ways harmful to others.

ALTRUISTIC INTENTION (BODHICHITTA) The mind dedicated to attaining enlightenment in order to be able to benefit all others most effectively.

ARHAT A person who has attained liberation and is thus free from cyclic existence.

ATTACHMENT An emotion that, based on exaggerating the good qualities of a person or thing, clings to it.

BASIS OF DESIGNATION The collection of parts or qualities in dependence upon which an object is labeled.

BODHICHITTA See Altruistic intention.

BODHISATTVA A person who, when seeing any sentient being, spontaneously feels the altruistic intention.

BUDDHA Any person who has purified all defilements and developed all good qualities. "The Buddha" refers to Shakyamuni Buddha, who lived 2,500 years ago in India.

BUDDHA-NATURE (BUDDHA-POTENTIAL) The factors allowing all beings to attain full enlightenment.

COMPASSION The wish for all sentient beings to be free from suffering and its causes.

CYCLIC EXISTENCE Taking uncontrolled rebirth under the influence of afflictions and karma.

DEITY (YIDAM) A meditational deity, one of a number of Buddhas.

DETERMINATION TO BE FREE (RENUNCIATION) The attitude aspiring to be free from all problems and sufferings and to attain liberation.

DHARMA The realizations and cessations of suffering and its causes. In a more general sense, Dharma refers to the teachings and doctrine of the Buddha.

DHARMA PROTECTOR   Dharma protectors may be either (1) an arya bodhisattva who manifests in a fierce aspect in order to protect the Dharma in our minds and our world, or (2) an ordinary being who is a spirit who has made a promise to a high lama to protect the Dharma. The first are considered to be supramundane protectors; the second are worldly protectors.

EMPTINESS   The lack of independent, or inherent, existence. This is the ultimate nature or reality of all persons and phenomena.

ENLIGHTENMENT (BUDDHAHOOD)   The state of a Buddha, that is, the state of having forever eliminated all disturbing attitudes, karmic imprints, and their stains from one's mindstream, and having developed one's good qualities and wisdom to their fullest extent. Buddhahood supersedes liberation.

IMPUTE   To give a label or name to an object. To give meaning to an object.

INHERENT OR INDEPENDENT EXISTENCE   A false and non-existent quality that we project onto persons and phenomena; existence independent of causes and conditions, parts, or the mind labeling a phenomena.

KARMA   Intentional action. Our actions leave imprints on our mindstreams that bring about our experiences.

LIBERATION   The state of having removed all afflictions and karma causing us to take rebirth in cyclic existence.

LOVE   The wish for all sentient beings to have happiness and its causes.

MAHAYANA   The Buddhist tradition that asserts all beings can attain enlightenment. It strongly emphasizes the development of compassion and the altruistic intention.

MANTRA   A series of syllables consecrated by a Buddha and expressing the essence of the entire path to enlightenment. Mantras can be recited during meditation to calm and purify the mind.

MEDITATION   Habituating ourselves to positive attitudes, beneficial emotions, and accurate perspectives.

MEDITATIVE QUIESCENCE The ability to remain single-pointedly on an object of meditation with a pliant and serene mind.

NIRVANA The cessation of suffering and its causes. Freedom from cyclic existence.

POSITIVE POTENTIAL Imprints of positive actions that will result in happiness in the future.

PURE LAND A place established by a Buddha or bodhisattva where all conditions are conducive for practicing the Dharma and attaining enlightenment.

REALIZATION A deep understanding that becomes part of us and changes our outlook on the world. When we realize love, for example, the way we feel about and relate to others changes dramatically.

SADHANA The meditational practice associated with a particular Buddha. This is often a written text that one follows, by chanting or reading, in order to meditate on that Buddha.

SANGHA Any person who directly and non-conceptually realizes emptiness. In a more general sense, Sangha refers to the communities of ordained monastics. It is sometimes used to refer to Buddhists in general.

SELFLESSNESS See Emptiness.

SPECIAL INSIGHT (VIPASHYANA) A wisdom thoroughly discriminating phenomena. When conjoined with meditative quiescence, it enables one to analyze the meditation object and simultaneously remain single-pointedly on it.

SPIRIT An unenlightened being born in the hungry ghost or demi-god (asura) realms. Spirits may be helpful or harmful.

SUFFERING (DUKKHA) Any dissatisfactory condition. It doesn't refer only to physical or mental pain, but includes all problematic conditions.

SUTRA A teaching of the Buddha; a Buddhist scripture. Sutras are found in all Buddhist traditions.

TAKING REFUGE Entrusting one's spiritual development to the guidance of the Three Jewels: the Buddha, Dharma, and Sangha.

TANTRA A scripture describing Vajrayana practice.

THREE HIGHER TRAININGS   The practices of ethics, meditative concentration, and wisdom. Practicing these three results in liberation.

THREE JEWELS   The Buddha, Dharma, and Sangha.

THREE PRINCIPAL REALIZATIONS (THREE PRINCIPAL ASPECTS) OF THE PATH   The determination to be free, the altruistic intention, and the wisdom realizing emptiness.

VAJRAYANA   A Mahayana Buddhist tradition popular in Tibet and Japan.

WISDOM REALIZING REALITY   A wisdom that correctly understands the manner in which all persons and phenomena exist, that is, the mind realizing the emptiness of inherent existence.

Additional Reading

Berzin, Alexander. *Relating to a Spiritual Teacher: Building a Healthy Relationship*. Ithaca, N.Y.: Snow Lion Publications, 2000.

Bokar Rinpoche. *Tara: The Feminine Divine*. San Francisco: Clear Point Press, 1999.

Chodron, Thubten. *Blossoms of the Dharma: Living as a Buddhist Nun*. Berkeley: North Atlantic Books, 2000.

Chodron, Thubten. *Buddhism for Beginners*. Ithaca, N.Y.: Snow Lion Publications, 2001.

Chodron, Thubten. *Open Heart, Clear Mind*. Ithaca, N.Y.: Snow Lion Publications, 1990.

Chodron, Thubten. *Taming the Mind*. Ithaca, N.Y.: Snow Lion Publications, 2004.

Chodron, Thubten. *Working with Anger*. Ithaca, N.Y.: Snow Lion Publications, 2001.

Dhammananda, K. Sri. *How to Live Without Fear and Worry*. Kuala Lumpur: Buddhist Missionary Society, 1989.

Dharmarakshita. *Wheel of Sharp Weapons*. Dharamsala, India: Library of Tibetan Works and Archives, 1981.

Gehlek Rinpoche and Brenda Rosen. *The Tara Box*. Novato, Calif.: New World Library, 2004.

Hanh, Thich Nhat. *Being Peace*. Berkeley: Parallax Press, 1987.

H. H. Tenzin Gyatso, the Fourteenth Dalai Lama. *The Dalai Lama at Harvard*. Ithaca, N.Y.: Snow Lion Publications, 1989.

H. H. Tenzin Gyatso, the Fourteenth Dalai Lama. *Kindness, Clarity and Insight*. Ithaca, N.Y.: Snow Lion Publications, 1984.

H. H. the Dalai Lama, Tsong-ka-pa, and Jeffrey Hopkins. *Deity Yoga*. Ithaca, N.Y.: Snow Lion Publications, 1981.

Jampa Tegchok, Geshe. *Transforming the Heart: The Buddhist Way to Joy and Courage*. Ithaca, N.Y.: Snow Lion Publications, 1999.

McDonald, Kathleen. *How to Meditate*. Boston: Wisdom Publications, 1984.

Rabten, Geshe, and Geshe Ngawang Dhargyey. *Advice from a Spiritual Friend*. Boston: Wisdom Publications, 1986.

Thubten Yeshe, Lama. *Introduction to Tantra*. Boston: Wisdom Publications, 1987.

Thubten Zopa Rinpoche, Lama. *The Door to Satisfaction*. Boston: Wisdom Publications, 1994.

Thubten Zopa Rinpoche, Lama. *Transforming Problems: Utilizing Happiness and Suffering in the Spiritual Path*. Boston: Wisdom Publications, 1987.

Trungpa, Chogyam. *Cutting Through Spiritual Materialism*. London: Shambhala Publications, 1973.

Tsomo, Karma Lekshe, ed. *Daughters of the Buddha*, Ithaca, N.Y.: Snow Lion Publications, 1988.

Tsongkhapa, Je. *The Three Principal Aspects of the Path*. Howell, N.J.: Mahayana Sutra and Tantra Press, 1988.

Wangchen, Geshe. *Awakening the Mind of Enlightenment*. Boston: Wisdom Publications, 1988.

Willis, Janice D., ed. *Feminine Ground*. Ithaca, N.Y.: Snow Lion Publications, 1987.

Willson, Martin. *In Praise of Tara*. Boston: Wisdom Publications, 1986.